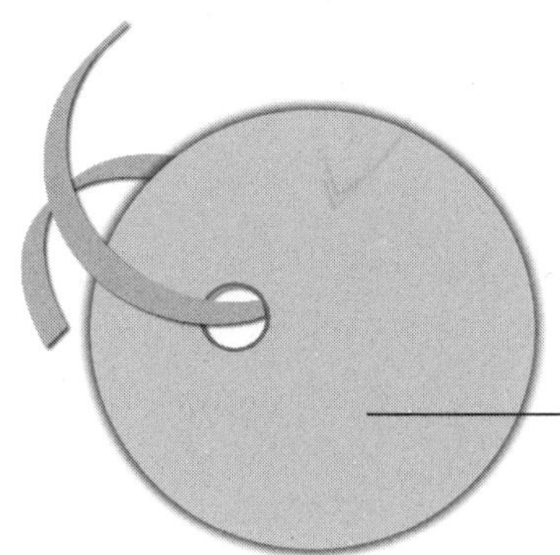

Contents

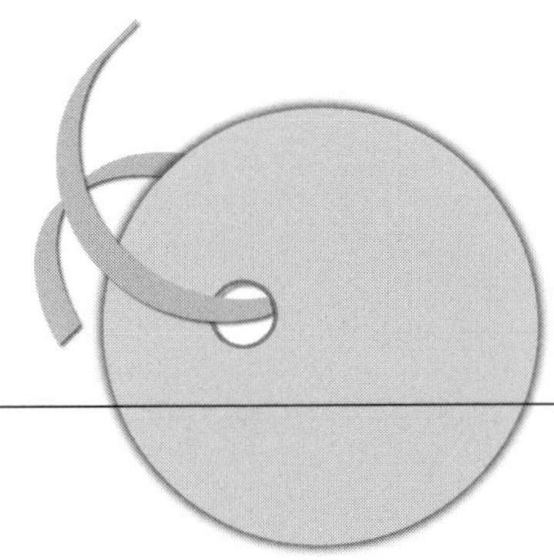

Introduction

This home-study guide will help children, teenagers and young adults learn the art of traditional English grammar, so that they can:

- write and speak better English
- think clearly and analytically
- learn another language more easily
- improve their communication skills for the job world.

It assumes that the student uses English as a first language or, if not, that the student is a confident, fluent user of English. Each new topic starts with a lesson and examples, followed by exercises for practice. The first few pages of the book are written in a simple style for late primary and early secondary children to handle, but then the work progresses to a more detailed, more advanced level for teenagers and young adults. The guide should be worked through from front to back, as later lessons assume that earlier work has been understood and mastered.

Beyond the grammar section of the book, the focus moves to punctuation and then to writing technique and good composition — important skills that take years of practice. Following this is a phonics summary. For ESL learners, and for students who need extra help with spelling and reading, the phonics list should be a helpful guide.

As well as grammar and composition, the other great teacher of eloquent communication is the reading of great books. Therefore, a general reading list has been included towards the back of the book. By studying the best examples of world literature, the student can gradually learn by example and should also show a big improvement in vocabulary and comprehension. Classical novels are rarely studied at school these days, but if students make the effort to read some of the books on the reading list, they are bound to reap big rewards for their efforts. At the end of the book are revision exercises, plus answers to all the exercises.

Learning the art of grammar not only helps improve communication skills, but is also a great exercise for the brain, in the same way that studying Maths, Science or Latin is. Grammar is analytical and requires the student to look at the purpose and function of each word, or group of words, in a sentence. To be able to parse or analyse a sentence correctly, the grammar student must be able to think logically and clearly. Learning grammar helps to discipline the mind and prevent sloppy thinking.

If you are learning a foreign language, understanding English grammar is 'half the battle'. Having a knowledge of such things as person, number, gender, case, tense, declensions and conjugations in English automatically helps the student grasp the same concepts in the new language.

To the children, teenagers and young adults who use this book, I hope you enjoy your study of grammar, and I wish you success in your journey towards better communication and a more disciplined mind. Your knowledge of grammar should give you extra confidence in yourself, help you in your secondary and post-secondary studies, and improve your chances of employment and promotion in your chosen career.

Parts of speech

The first thing you learn when you study grammar is the different parts of speech. Different types of words have different jobs to do. Some are naming words, some are action words, some describe things, others join or relate groups of words. All these different types of words are called the 'parts of speech'. Parts of speech include nouns, verbs, adjectives, adverbs, pronouns, prepositions, conjunctions, articles and interjections. Here is a brief summary of them:

- **Nouns** are naming words. They give the names of people, places, things, feelings and ideas (e.g. girl, man, John, Mrs Smith, beach, Africa, pencil, book, heat, hunger, health).
- **Pronouns** stand in the place of nouns. Once a noun has already been used, a pronoun can be used to represent that noun (e.g. she, it, they, us, I, mine, his, theirs, somebody, everyone).
- **Adjectives** are describing words. They describe nouns and pronouns (e.g. pretty, clever, dirty, happy, hot, fantastic, five, yellow, American).
- **Verbs** are doing, being and having words. They tell what action is happening (e.g. run, jump, think, sleep, write, am, are, is, was, were, have, has, had).
- **Adverbs** are modifying words. They usually modify verbs, telling how, where and when. They can also modify adjectives and other adverbs, telling how much (e.g. angrily, sadly, slowly, over, up, yesterday, soon, very, hardly, rarely).
- **Conjunctions** are joining words. They join one part of a sentence to another (e.g. but, and, because, although, until, unless, if).
- **Prepositions** are relating words. They relate a noun or pronoun in the first part of the sentence with a noun or pronoun in the second part. They often tell about position (e.g. under, over, inside, above, to, at, for, with, on, by, beneath).
- **Articles** are specifying words. They tell whether a noun is definite and specific, or indefinite and non-specific ('the' is the definite article; 'a' and 'an' are the indefinite articles).
- **Interjections** are words that show strong feeling, shock or surprise. They are followed by exclamation marks (e.g. Wow! Crikey! Golly! Gee wizz! Blimey! Oh no! Strewth! No way!).

1

Nouns

What are they?

Nouns are naming words.

They give the names of people, places, things, feelings and ideas.

Examples of nouns are:

<u>People</u>: Angela, Kevin, Mrs Carter, Dr Dolittle, Queen Victoria, girl, man, teacher, nurse

<u>Places</u>: Hyde Park, Korea, Washington, the River Nile, the Himalayas, beach, park, forest

<u>Things</u>: peg, pencil, rubbish, grass, cup, book, computer, window, car, Gameboy, Nintendo

<u>Feelings</u>: hunger, thirst, tiredness, happiness, sorrow, fear, anger, love, hope, boredom

<u>Ideas</u>: education, politics, health, sport, travel, biology, government, slavery, intelligence

Types of nouns

Nouns come in four varieties: common, proper, collective and abstract.

- **Common nouns** are the names of ordinary things that you can see and touch. The following words are examples of common nouns: egg, duck, man, river, soup, shoe, girl, rat, carrot. See if you can think of some more.
- **Proper nouns** are the names of special people, places and events. They are always spelt with capital letters. These are examples of proper nouns: Mr Smith, Father Christmas, the Queen, Australia, Samantha, the Amazon River, Easter, the Sydney Harbour Bridge. Now you think of some.
- **Collective nouns** are the names of collections or groups of people, animals and objects. Here are some collective nouns: herd, crowd, group, flock, congregation, audience, fleet, bunch, pack. Give some more examples.
- **Abstract nouns** are the names of feelings and ideas. They are not things that you can see and touch. Look at the following examples: dream, terror, hunger, fear, happiness, fun, education, punishment, sympathy. Now think of some of your own.

Have a GO! Ans p.101

Put the following nouns into their correct columns in the table below:

Mrs Lee, star, saucer, beauty, group, horror, egg, Britain, boys, sport, misery, heat, sardines, democracy, the King of Spain, king, dog, Monty, fleet, Bondi, crowd, wealth, class, fish, mob, Perth, Wizard of Oz, apple, desk, gang, comedy, Kelloggs.

Common	Proper	Collective	Abstract

Collective nouns

Most collective nouns are linked to a **particular group** of people, animals, plants or objects. When using good English, it is important to use the correct collective noun.

Look at the examples below and see how many you already know. Study the ones you don't know, so you can use them correctly in future:

an audience of listeners	a colony of penguins	a pride of lions
a murder of ravens	a choir of singers	a spool of thread
a congregation of worshippers	a pack of wolves/cards	a litter of puppies
a brood of chickens	a board of directors	a bouquet of flowers
a crowd of people	a fleet of ships	an ambush of tigers
a swarm of bees	a class of pupils	a batch of scones
a band of musicians	a galaxy of stars	a flock of birds/sheep
a gaggle of geese	a pod of whales	a cluster of diamonds
a company of actors	a collection of stamps	a herd of cattle
a plague of locusts	a school of fish	a battery of weapons
a gang of thieves/hoodlums	a ream of paper	a parliament of owls

Singular and plural nouns

Nouns have **number**. They can be singular (when there is only **one**) or plural (when there is **more than one**). Number is usually shown in nouns by the **ending on the word**.

How to turn singulars into plurals

To turn singular nouns into plurals, it is usually only necessary to add an 's' or 'es' to the end of the singular noun:

- Most nouns just add an 's' for the plural: dog, dogs; room, rooms; ant, ants.
- Nouns ending in 'ss', 'sh', 'ch' or 'x' use an 'es' in the plural: dress, dresses; kiss, kisses; dish, dishes; lunch, lunches; peach, peaches; box, boxes; fox, foxes.

However, sometimes there are a few other rules you need to follow:

- If a noun ends in **'y' with a consonant** just before it, change the 'y' into 'i' before adding 'es': baby, babies; lady, ladies; daddy, daddies; puppy, puppies.
- If a noun ends in **'y' with a vowel** just before it, such as 'ey', just add an 's': monkey, monkeys; journey, journeys; guy, guys; day, days; boy, boys.
- If a noun ends in **'f' or 'fe'**, the 'f' is *usually* changed to a 'v' before adding 'es': wharf, wharves; life, lives; wife, wives; dwarf, dwarves; knife, knives.
- When a noun ends in **'o'**, an 'es' is *usually* added: tomato, tomatoes; hero, heroes; mango, mangoes; potato, potatoes; tornado, tornadoes; volcano, volcanoes.
- When a **musical or shortened noun** ends in an 'o', just add 's': cello, cellos; piccolo, piccolos; photo, photos; memo, memos. Also note: zero, zeros.
- Some nouns have strange plurals that just have to be learnt: ox, oxen; child, children; foot, feet; louse, lice; woman, women; goose, geese.
- Some nouns are the same in the singular and plural: salmon, salmon; trout, trout; deer, deer; moose, moose; sheep, sheep.

Nouns from Latin and Greek

Many English words have come from the ancient languages of Latin and Greek, and some still have their Latin or Greek endings, especially scientific words. Look at how their singulars are turned into plurals:

Singular ending	Latin or Greek plural
'us' as in radius	'i' as in radii
'um' as in medium	'a' as in media
'is' as in oasis	'es' as in oases
'a' as in alga	'ae' as in algae
'on' as in phenomenon	'a' as in phenomena
'ex' as in index	'ices' as in indices
'ix' as in appendix	'ices' as in appendices

Have a GO! Ans p.101

On the left are some singular nouns. Write in their plurals on the right side:

Singular noun	Plural noun
dog	
cat	
peach	
fox	
puppy	
journey	
dwarf	
wife	
mango	
tomato	
potato	
vertex	
bacterium	

Singular noun	Plural noun
crisis	
hippopotamus	
deer	
sheep	
ox	
piano	
zero	
photo	
house	
foot	
tooth	
child	
mouse	

Change the following so that the singular sentences become plural, and the plural ones become singular:

1 The boy is riding his bike up a very steep hill.

2 The women go to the oases with their oxen and camels to fetch water.

3 The deer and sheep must be protected from the wolves in the woods.

4 I have a box with a peach, a mango, a photo and a shark's tooth in it.

5 This book has an appendix at the back.

6 A rhombus is like a pushed-over square.

Gender of nouns

Nouns come in **four genders**:

- **Masculine** gender is for male nouns, such as father, bull, boy, man, king, uncle.
- **Feminine** gender is for female nouns, such as queen, girl, woman, cow, hen, lady.
- **Neuter** gender is for neutral things, such as box, grass, pen, sink, egg, tap, bike.
- **Common** gender is used when there is a mixture of male and female, such as people, parents, children, animals, cattle, fish.

Have a look at the list of masculine and feminine nouns below. See how many you know and learn the ones you don't know.

Masculine	Feminine	Masculine	Feminine
man	woman	lord	lady
boy	girl	knight	dame
father	mother	conductor	conductress
son	daughter	waiter	waitress
brother	sister	actor	actress
husband	wife	master	mistress
uncle	aunt	manager	manageress
nephew	niece	god	goddess
emperor	empress	aviator	aviatrix
king	queen	policeman	policewoman
prince	princess	hero	heroine
duke	duchess	wizard	witch

Have a GO!

Ans p.102

Below are some masculine nouns. Without copying from the list above, put in their feminine equivalents:

Masculine	Feminine	Masculine	Feminine
king		uncle	
prince		man	
duke		husband	
knight		actor	
lord		waiter	
emperor		master	
wizard		aviator	
hero		conductor	
manager		god	

Adults and their young

Many living things have a name for the adult and another for their offspring.

Look at the list below and see how many adults and babies you know. Also, notice the column showing the common name. This is used when you think about these living things in general. As before, once you have studied and learnt these words, have a go at the exercise that follows, without looking back at this list:

Common	Father	Mother	Baby
dog	dog	bitch	pup
cat	tomcat	cat	kitten
fowl	rooster/cockerel	hen	chicken
duck	drake	duck	duckling
goose	gander	goose	gosling
swan	cob	swan	cygnet
bird	bird	bird	nestling/fledgling
frog	frog	frog	tadpole
pig	boar	sow	piglet
cattle	bull	cow	calf
horse	stallion	mare	foal
deer	stag	doe	fawn
sheep	ram	ewe	lamb
goat	billy-goat	nanny-goat	kid
lion	lion	lioness	cub
tiger	tiger	tigress	cub
fox	fox	vixen	cub
wolf	wolf	she-wolf	cub
whale	bull whale	whale cow	whale calf
elephant	bull elephant	elephant cow	elephant calf
human	man	woman	baby/child
tree	tree	tree	sapling
plant	plant	plant	seedling
flower	flower	flower	bud

Ans p.102

On the left are some adult nouns. Put their babies on the right.

Adult	Baby	Adult	Baby
sheep		swan	
dog		hen	
duck		pig	
goose		cow	
cat		whale	
deer		human	
horse		plant	
bird		tree	
goat		flower	

Pronouns

What are they?

Pronouns are words that you can use **instead of nouns**, so that you don't have to repeat the same noun over and over again.

Examples of pronouns are:

I, me, you, he, she, it, we, they, us, them, him, hers, mine, ours, its, either, each, no one, somebody, myself, who, which, that.

The following paragraph shows what it would sound like if we didn't use pronouns. It sounds horrible.

Jenny is a schoolgirl. Jenny is six years old and Jenny goes to Chatswood Public School, where Jenny is in Year 1. Jenny has a big brother called Mark. Mark is twelve and Mark loves cricket. Mark's favourite food is noodles and Mark also loves going to the cinema.

Have a GO! Ans p.102

1 Put some pronouns in the paragraph above to make it sound better. I'll start it off for you:

Jenny is a schoolgirl. She is six years old and ...

GO!

2 Underline all the pronouns you can see in the following sentences:

a Stephen hit his head on the bar, but it didn't hurt him.

b You should go to the doctor if you are sick, and he will cure you.

c The teacher gave Leon a detention because he was so naughty.

d This book is mine, that is yours and those are theirs.

e We could go and visit them after our lesson.

f Nobody told me that it was your birthday.

g The boy, who lives down the road, likes to throw mud pies.

Types of pronouns

1 **Personal** pronouns refer to people and things:
He is coming to my place today.
We went to the beach with them.
She gave it a shake.

2 **Possessive** pronouns show possession:
This is mine and that is yours.
These roller blades are his.

3 **Demonstrative** pronouns point things out:
This is the way to the shops and that is the way home.
These are mine and those are yours.

4 **Interrogative** pronouns ask questions:
Who is coming with me?
What is the time?
Which is Tom's desk?

5 **Relative** pronouns relate one thing to another:
The biscuits, which we ate this morning, were supposed to be for the party.
The tiger snake that chased the boys is hiding behind the bushes.
The professor, whom we met yesterday, has just invented a time-machine.

6 **Reflexive** pronouns show the action is done by the doer to himself or herself:
I wash myself in the mornings.
They tested themselves before the exams.

7 **Reciprocal** pronouns show the action is swapped between the doers:
They lied to each other.
Members of the team shouted at one another.

8 **Emphatic** pronouns emphasise who does the action:
He did it himself, so he should be very proud.
I, myself, will be there to give the speech.

9 **Distributive** pronouns show how things are shared or distributed:
Each of us has ten books.
Neither of the children could find the hidden eggs.
None of the boys had been here before.

10 **Indefinite** pronouns refer to people generally, not specifically:
They say she was a wicked witch.
Nobody knows where she went.
One should be very careful when walking on thin ice.

Pronoun or adjective?

Some words look just like possessive, demonstrative, interrogative and distributive pronouns, but they are actually possessive, demonstrative, interrogative and distributive **adjectives**. Their purpose is to describe the nouns that follow them. (See Chapter 3 for more about adjectives.)

Remember that a pronoun takes the place of a noun. If a noun follows a 'pronoun', that 'pronoun' is actually an adjective:

- Will you take my dog for a walk? (possessive adjective)
- These guitars belonged to the Beatles. (demonstrative adjective)
- Which skateboard belongs to you? (interrogative adjective)
- Neither girl entered the trampoline competition. (distributive adjective)

Have a GO! Ans p.102

Look at the underlined pronouns below and state what kind they are:

1 This is the bully, and that is his victim. ______
2 You, yourself, should know not to do that. ______
3 Wendy burnt herself badly on the stove. ______
4 Haelynn said she was sorry. ______
5 Everyone in the class has Derwent pencils. ______
6 The dog that lives next door is very old. ______
7 What is that terrible noise? ______
8 Neither of them knew what each other was doing. ______
9 The whale, which has just had a baby, has swum out to sea.
______
10 They always tell you to look both ways. ______
11 That is mine. ______
12 Which is my cup? ______
13 She asked if I could read to him. ______
______
14 They fed themselves before they went out. ______

3

Adjectives

What are they?

Adjectives are **describing words**. They describe nouns and pronouns.

Examples of adjectives are:

The fierce lion let out a frightening roar, and all the terrified animals ran for their lives. They were nice and fat and juicy, just right for a lion's dinner. That's how he saw it, anyway.

Adjectives come before nouns (pretty *girl*) and after verbs of being and sensing (I *am* twelve; this *tastes* good).

Have a GO! Ans p.102

1 On the left are some nouns. Think of a good adjective to go with each one, to give it a description:

Noun	Adjective	Noun	Adjective
boy		circus	
mouse		monster	
lion		holiday	
teacher		volcano	
dream		dinner	
planet		dinosaur	

2 Now underline all the adjectives you see in the following sentences:

It was a wild and windy night and, as the wispy clouds sailed across the rising, yellow moon, I saw an ugly witch riding a bristly broomstick, her tall, pointed hat on her head and a black cat with shining eyes resting on her shoulder. I could hear the witch's evil cackle as she flew off into the cold, midnight air.

Types of adjectives

There are six types of adjectives. The two main types are descriptive and limiting adjectives, but pronouns can be used as adjectives as well:

1. Those that describe a noun are **descriptive** adjectives: a red dress, a happy face, a scary monster, a big balloon, a sad story, a tasty meal.
2. Those that limit a noun are **limiting** adjectives: the first day, five eggs, the least amount, the last race, the earlier train, enough sugar.
3. Those that show possession of a noun are **possessive** adjectives: my toy, their shoes, our house, your work.
4. Those that point out a noun are **demonstrative** adjectives: those skis, these snowboards, this hat, that dress.
5. Those that ask questions about a noun are **interrogative** adjectives: whose watch? which book? what pencil?
6. Those that show how nouns are distributed are **distributive** adjectives: neither boy, each video, every computer.

Notice that possessive, demonstrative, interrogative and distributive **adjectives are followed by nouns,** whereas possessive, demonstrative, interrogative and distributive **pronouns stand alone,** without a noun.

Ans p.102

In this exercise underline the adjectives in the sentences and state what type they are. Also put a circle around the nouns they describe:

1. The heavy rain spoilt the day. ____________________
2. My former teacher was very strict, but my present one is more lenient.

   ____
3. The first child to talk will be given a detention. ____________________
4. Ants are very small, but also very powerful. ____________________
5. Eight girls came to the party. ____________________
6. The pupil who writes with the most clarity will win the prize. ____________________
7. The hot mud bubbled near the volcano. ____________________
8. Your writing is very untidy. ____________________
9. Every boy in the class plays soccer. ____________________
10. These boxes need to be put in the storeroom. ____________________
11. Which puppy do you think is the cutest? ____________________

4

Verbs

What are they?

Verbs are doing, being and having words.

- The **doing** words tell about the **action** happening in the sentence.
- The **being** and **having** words usually help with verb **tense**, telling when the action happened. Being words also tell how something **is**, and having words tell what someone **has**.

Examples of doing words are:

Lauren jumped into the pool.
Jack will drive the car to school.
That man smokes a pipe.

Examples of having words are:

I have all the ingredients for the recipe.
Gloria has a brother and sister.
In the old days, people had lots of children.
Tony will have a great time at the show.

Examples of being words are:

I am twelve years old.
Jenny and Ken are from Taiwan.
We were at the beach this morning.
I have been in bed with the flu.
David and Paul will be home at noon.
Harry is the naughtiest boy in the class.

Have a GO! Ans p.103

See if you can underline the verbs in the sentences and say whether they are doing, being or having words. For example: I swim every day in summer. (doing)

1 Bill skis at Thredbo when he has the money. ________________

2 Tim is from Korea. ________________

3 Judy is a hard-working student. ________________

4 Max does maths every day. ________________

5 Rebecca has a pretty face. ________________

6 Helen is a tomboy. ________________

7 Daniel should be here by ten o'clock. ____________________

8 I skipped, Leonie hopped and Haelynn jumped along the footpath. ____________

9 I sleep in a big bed. ____________________

10 If you study hard, you will pass the exam. ____________________

Tenses of verbs

All verbs have **tense**:

- If the action happens now, the verb is in the **present** tense.
- If the action has finished, it is in the **past** tense.
- If the action hasn't happened yet, it is in the **future** tense.

Examples of the **present tense** are:

Cathy plays with Jim today. (present simple tense)

Cathy is playing with Jim today. (present continuous tense)

Examples of the **past tense** are:

Cathy played with Jim yesterday. (past simple tense)

Cathy was playing with Jim yesterday. (past continuous tense)

Examples of the **future tense** are:

Cathy will play with Jim tomorrow. (future simple tense)

Cathy will be playing with Jim tomorrow. (future continuous tense)

Notice that the continuous tense uses the verb 'to be' in front of the action word (am going, was singing), whereas the simple tense uses the action word alone (go, sang).

Have a GO! Ans p.103

See if you can work out whether the underlined verbs in the following sentences are present, past or future, and whether they are simple or continuous.

For example: I am going to the Christmas party. (present, continuous)

1 Tina likes noodles. ____________________

2 Benn ran all the way to the shops. ____________________

3 Adam was walking in the bush, when he fell over. ____________________

4 Bill will do his reading when he goes to bed. ____________________

5 Toko will be playing in the garden, when you arrive. ____________________

6 We are coming first in the competition. ____________________

GO!

7 James dropped his dinner all over the floor. ______________________

8 Gloria will go to the shops with her sister Grace. ______________________

____

9 Skye and Simon were playing with the little, yellow duckling. ______________________

____

10 Tim will be furious if he finds out what you did. ______________________

____

Perfect tense

Just as the continuous tense uses the verb 'to be' in front of the action word (is going, was playing, are waiting), the **perfect tense** uses the verb 'to have' in front of the action word (has gone, had played, have waited).

Have a GO! Ans p.103

See if you can fill in the blanks below, using the correct form of the verb.

Present	Past	Perfect	Future
have	had	have had	will
am/are	was/were	have	will be
go		have gone	will go
do	did	have	will do
make		have made	will
take		have	will take
shake		have	will shake
stand		have	will stand
weep		have wept	will
sleep	slept	have	will
creep		have crept	will creep
leap	leapt	have	will leap
dream		have	will dream
swim		have	will
sing	sang	have	will sing
sink	sank	have	will
stink		have stunk	will stink
drink		have	will drink
think		have thought	will think
buy		have	will buy
bring		have	will
write		have written	will write
say		have said	will say
lie	lay	have	will
lay	laid	have	will
draw		have drawn	will draw

Present	Past	Perfect	Future
know		have known	will know
blow		have	will
throw		have	will throw
show	showed	have	will show
run		have run	will
speak		have spoken	will speak
strike		have struck	will
eat		have eaten	will eat
see		have seen	will see
put		have put	will put
shut		have shut	will
sew	sewed	have	will sew
mean		have meant	will mean
hide	hid	have	will hide
drive	drove	have	will
ride	rode	have	will ride
slide		have slid	will
sit		have sat	will

Conjugating verbs

A verb conjugation is a list that shows **how a verb changes** in the various tenses. Some verbs follow a simple pattern for present, past and perfect tenses, whereas other verbs change their form dramatically. Those that follow a regular pattern are called **regular verbs** and have regular (weak) conjugations. Verbs that change form in the different tenses are called **irregular verbs** and have irregular (strong) conjugations. Examples of regular and irregular conjugations are shown below:

Regular (weak) conjugation

Pronoun	Present	Past simple	Perfect
I	jump	jumped	have jumped
You (singular)	jump	jumped	have jumped
He/she/it	jumps	jumped	has jumped
We	jump	jumped	have jumped
You (plural)	jump	jumped	have jumped
They	jump	jumped	have jumped

Irregular (strong) conjugation

Pronoun	Present	Past simple	Perfect
I	am	was	have been
You (singular)	are	were	have been
He/she/it	is	was	has been
We	are	were	have been
You (plural)	are	were	have been
They	are	were	have been

Have a GO! Ans p.104

Try to use the correct form of the verb (shown in brackets) in the sentences below:

1 If you had (be) __________ here, this would never have (happen) ____________.

2 I (go) __________ to the shops very early, so that it wouldn't be too crowded.

3 She has (drive) _____________ them to the beach, so they won't be back till this afternoon.

4 I was so tired that I (lie) ________ down for a sleep.

5 I (bring) ____________ a chair from home, but he (buy) ___________ a brand new one from the shops. (past simple)

6 The hen has just (lay) _________ a beautiful brown egg, and now she has (lie) __________ down to have a rest.

7 The burglar (hide) _____________ behind the bushes and (wait) ____________ for the people to leave their house. (past simple)

8 I have (make) __________ up my mind to tell them the truth about what really happened.

9 Today he (say) __________ it is hard, but yesterday he (say) ________ that it was easy.

10 The cat didn't (eat) _______ the fish last night, but he (eat) ________ it last week, and he has (eat) ______________ fish many times before.

11 We have (have) __________ enough to drink, and you have (sleep) ________ for long enough now.

Have a GO! Ans p.104

First, turn these sentences from present simple into past simple, and then put them into the perfect tense.

1 We always go to the shops on Saturdays.

2 He plays football with the Gordon Soccer Club.

3 I write letters to my friends in England.

4 You drive like a maniac!

5 The hens lay eggs almost every day.

6 She lies down, if she has a headache.

7 It is not necessary to ring me.

8 I can come to your place on Saturday.

9 Students concentrate better if they eat breakfast before school.

10 The volcano in New Zealand blows its top every few years.

5

Adverbs

What are they?

Just as adjectives describe nouns, and give them more detail, adverbs do the same with verbs. Adverbs **add** to the **verb**, as it says in the word.

- Adverbs tell **how**, **where**, **when** or **how much** about the verb.
- Sometimes, adverbs also describe adjectives and other adverbs.

Examples of adverbs are:

When James came over yesterday, it was really cold, so we chopped some wood quickly and sat cosily by the fireside, playing Monopoly and drinking hot chocolate.

Types of adverbs

1 Adverbs of **manner** tell **how** something is done. They usually end in 'ly':

I bent [verb] over slowly [adverb], because I had a sore back.

2 Adverbs of **time** tell **when** something is done:

Because you arrived [verb] late [adverb], you missed the train.

3 Adverbs of **place** tell **where** something is done:

The boys were kept [verb] inside [adverb], because they were naughty.

4 Adverbs of **quantity** tell **how much** something is done or something is like. They often describe adjectives and other adverbs, as well as verbs:

We really [adverb] enjoyed [verb] the bushwalk, although we were absolutely [adverb] exhausted [adjective].

Have a GO! Ans p.104

1 See if you can spot the adverbs in the following sentences and underline them. Also say whether they tell how, how much, where or when about the verb.

For example: Kim came to my place yesterday. (when)

a Tomorrow is my birthday. ____________________

b Nasser can run faster than Ken. ____________________

c The drunk driver crashed violently into the tree. ____________________

d The taxi drove too slowly and we were very late. ____________________

e The sun came up, and the birds started to sing sweetly. ____________________

f In maths, if you get behind, it's hard to catch up. ____________________

g The thief crept quietly into the room. ____________________

h The snowman melted quickly in the hot sun. ____________________

i Peter spoke rudely to his mother, so he was punished. ____________________

j You were quite right to ignore the bully. ____________________

k The surgeon operated carefully and the patient was saved. ____________________

2 Some of these sentences have more than one adverb, so beware!
Circle the adverbs and underline the words they describe (modify).
Under each adverb, state whether it is one of time, manner, quantity or place:

a The children skipped cheerfully home from school.

____

b I feel miserable today. (Note: 'miserable' is an adjective. Find the adverb.)

____

c He worked slowly because he found it hard. (Note: 'hard' is an adjective. Find the adverb.)

____

d Today we are going nowhere.

____

e The petrol tank is almost empty.

____

f The wind howled spookily through the trees.

____

g The stars in the night sky looked incredibly beautiful.

____

h You never eat your vegetables.

____

i The mouse ran away, before the cat saw it.

____

6

Comparatives and superlatives

What are they?

When **making comparisons** between two or more things, comparative and superlative adjectives are used. Comparative and superlative adverbs are used when comparing verbs.

Examples of comparatives are:

Adam is the taller of the two brothers.
Jane is cleverer than Judy.
Peter is the more handsome of the two boys.

Examples of superlatives are:

Of the three sisters, she is the lightest.
Anna is the funniest girl I have ever known.
Angus is the most intelligent pupil in the class.

Comparative and superlative adjectives

The **comparative** is used to compare two things only.

- For short adjectives, the comparative form ends in 'er': big, bigger; short, shorter; pretty, prettier.
- For longer adjectives, the comparative form uses 'more' in front of the adjective: intelligent, more intelligent; fantastic, more fantastic.

The **superlative** is used to compare three or more things.

- For short adjectives, the superlative form ends in 'est': tight, tightest; funny, funniest; little, littlest.
- For longer adjectives, the superlative form uses 'most' in front of the adjective: beautiful, most beautiful; fortunate, most fortunate.

A few adjectives have **irregular** comparatives and superlatives, which follow no pattern:

- good, better, best
- bad, worse, worst
- much, more, most.

Double comparatives and superlatives

Remember that you must **never** use double comparatives or superlatives.

These days, many people say things such as 'most easiest' or 'more tastier'. The correct forms are 'easiest' and 'tastier', of course.

To help keep your own grammar in good shape, it is helpful to note people's mistakes when they speak. Don't correct the speaker's grammar out loud, as this is not polite, but correct their mistakes in your own mind. This will help you to continue speaking correctly and not to pick up the bad habits of others.

Have a GO! Ans p.104

Fill in the following table.

Positive	Comparative	Superlative
big		
small		
funny		
beautiful		
complicated		
good		
bad		
much		
little		

Comparative and superlative adverbs

When making comparisons with adverbs, adverbs ending in 'ly' are treated differently from those that don't end in 'ly'.

Adverbs that end in 'ly'

- For the comparative, use 'more' before the adverb: more quickly, more smoothly, more soundly.
- For the superlative, use 'most' before the adverb: most quickly, most smoothly, most soundly.

Adverbs that don't end in 'ly'

- Use 'er' for comparatives: sooner, later, faster.
- Use 'est' for superlatives: soonest, latest, fastest.

Examples

Look at the following comparatives:

She ran more quickly in the race than her sister did.

John sang more sweetly before his voice broke.

I can think faster than you can.

Look at the following superlatives:

He ran the most swiftly of all the boys.

Mrs Morgan explained it the most clearly of all the teachers.

Of the three girls, Jenny arrived the latest.

Confusion between adjectives and adverbs

People often confuse adjectives with adverbs, using an adjective when they should really be using an adverb. Remember that **adjectives describe nouns** (and pronouns), while **adverbs modify verbs** (and sometimes other adjectives or adverbs).

Please leave the room quietly.

'Quietly' is an adverb describing, or modifying, the verb 'leave'.

The boy was quiet while he was studying.

'Quiet' is an adjective describing the noun 'boy'.

I am really happy to see you.

'Really' is an adverb modifying the adjective 'happy'.

Ans p.104

Decide whether to use adjectives or adverbs in the sentences below by crossing out the incorrect words:

1 The man looked cold/coldly, standing in the rain.
2 The man looked cold/coldly at the child and walked away.
3 I feel awkward/awkwardly if someone stares at me.
4 I felt awkward/awkwardly in my pocket, searching for my bus ticket.

7

Conjunctions

What are they?

Conjunctions are **joining words**. They join one sentence to another. 'And', 'but' and 'than' are all conjunctions.

Examples of conjunctions are:

Jon has an apple. Jon has a book.
Jon has an apple <u>and</u> a book.
It rained. We went anyway.
It rained, <u>but</u> we went anyway.
Kim went up the hill. Kirstie went up the hill.
Kim <u>and</u> Kirstie went up the hill.
('went up the hill' in omitted after 'Kim' but is understood)
Justin runs. Peter runs faster.
Peter runs faster <u>than</u> Justin. ('runs' is omitted after 'Justin' but is understood)

Here are some other conjunctions: because, although, whenever, if, since, so, while, unless, that, until.

Conjunctions can be used in the middle of sentences, as shown above, or at the beginning of sentences:
<u>Unless</u> you have combed your hair, you won't be allowed to go out.
<u>While</u> you were out, the phone rang.
<u>Although</u> the tornado swept past, the house remained standing.

Ans p.104

Find and underline the conjunctions in the following sentences:

1 I looked everywhere, but I couldn't find it.

2 Mary ate a biscuit and Tom ate a cake.

3 We ran home because it was raining.

4 David sneezes whenever he is near a cat.

5 We stayed up late, although we were tired.

6 Your work has improved since you've been studying.

7 Gloria is smaller than Steven.

8 Although it is hot, let's go for a walk.

9 Whenever the birds are singing, I stop and listen.

10 William and Jason have scooters.

11 Because it was the holidays, the shops were closed.

12 Toko and Yoshi come from Japan.

13 There were black clouds in the sky, but it didn't rain.

14 The noise has stopped now, so we can relax.

Finding conjunctions

An easy way to spot conjunctions is to find **all the verbs** in a sentence, and then look for the smaller sentences linked to each verb. The conjunction/s that join the little sentences into a big sentence should now be easy to find. For example:

If (you <u>come</u> to my party,) (you <u>will get</u> cake). The conjunction is *if*.

Ans p.104

In the following sentences, underline each verb and notice how a little sentence forms around it. Then circle the conjunctions that join the little sentences into a longer one:

1 She didn't come, because she wasn't invited.

2 Whenever we go skiing, it rains.

3 She worked hard at maths and came top.

4 Although we wrote him a letter, he didn't reply.

5 They raced to get the washing in, but it still got wet.

6 You should have been told that it would cost a lot of money.

7 Haelynn and Jade must go to bed now.

8 Tina can come to the party, but not Ken.

9 They went on a bush walk, even though the sun was setting.

10 If you can find it, you can keep it.

11 I'm coming too, whether you like it or not.

12 Unless the boys get here by noon, they will miss the ferry.

13 While you were out, a parcel was delivered.

8 Interjections

What are they?

Interjections are words that are used to **show shock, surprise, delight or other strong feeling**. They can be one or two words long and are followed by an exclamation mark.

Examples of interjections are:

Gosh! Gee wiz! Fair dinkum! Wow! Strewth! Oh no! Good heavens! Blimey! Fantastic! Good grief!.

Exclamations

When **a whole sentence** shows shock, surprise or strong feeling, it is called an exclamation. It is also followed by an exclamation mark.

What a clever boy you are!
Don't ever do that again!

Have a GO! Ans p.104

Look at the following sentences, add punctuation marks where necessary, and state whether the sentences contain interjections, are examples of exclamations or are just ordinary statements or questions.

1 I've told you a million times not to do that ____________________

____

2 I get terrible hay fever in Spring ____________________

____

3 That was the best film I've ever seen ____________________

____

4 Fantastic your reading is really improving ____________________

____

5 Oh no I forgot to bring the present ______________________________

____

6 Have you done your Christmas shopping yet ______________________________

____

7 Brilliant I didn't know you could do that ______________________________

____

8 My favourite animals at the zoo are the wombats and the apes ______________

____

9

Prepositions

What are they?

Prepositions are **relating words**, which relate a noun or pronoun in the first part of the sentence with one in the second part. They often tell about **position**. Notice the word 'position' is hidden inside the word 'preposition'.

Examples of prepositions are:

in, out, up, over, under, beside, beyond, between, below, among, to, at, with, for.

Prepositions are nearly always followed by a noun or pronoun. This noun or pronoun is called the 'object of the preposition'.

Humpty Dumpty sat on the wall.

'Humpty Dumpty' (noun) is related to the 'wall' (noun) by the preposition 'on'.

Jack fell down the hill.

'Jack' (noun) is related to the 'hill' (noun) by the preposition 'down'.

Little Miss Muffet sat on her tuffet.

'Little Miss Muffet' (noun) is related to the 'tuffet' (noun) by the preposition 'on'.

Ans p.105

See if you can underline the prepositions in the following:

1 Jack jumped over the candlestick.

2 Mary took her lamb to school.

3 Josh had great big boots on his feet.

4 Jill hid among the bushes.

5 Bad men go to gaol.

6 The big, black clouds are in the sky.

GO!

7 I wake up at 7 o'clock.
8 The cat hid under the chair.
9 The boys crawled into the cupboard.
10 The cow jumped over the moon.
11 The soup is in the pot.
12 The elephant sat on my foot.
13 The sun set behind the mountains.
14 The dog with the long tail is mine.

Ending a sentence with a preposition

In traditional grammar, it is considered incorrect to end a sentence with a preposition, because a noun or pronoun is supposed to follow a preposition. However, today this rule is often not followed.

Who are you going to the beach with?

In traditional English the correct wording should be:

With whom are you going to the beach?

These days, many people think that this sounds stilted and too formal, especially in ordinary conversation. Use your own judgement. If you are writing formally, avoid ending sentences with prepositions. Bring them to the front of the sentence, as above. In everyday speech or writing, ignore the rule if the sentence sounds too stiff and unnatural.

10

Articles

What are they?

Articles are **types of adjectives** — they describe nouns by specifying them into **definite** and **indefinite** types:

Examples of articles are:

<u>the</u>, <u>a</u>, <u>an</u>.

- The **definite** article is 'the'. It is called 'definite' because it refers to a definite, specific person or thing already known about (the queen, the school, the girl).

  We bought <u>the</u> house on <u>the</u> corner.

- The **indefinite** article is 'a' before a word starting with a consonant (a book, a toy), or 'an' if it comes before a word starting with a vowel or silent 'h' (an egg, an hour). The indefinite articles refer to indefinite, non-specific people and things not already known about.

  Could you please lend me <u>a</u> pencil so I can write this note.

Native English speakers use articles correctly without thinking, but for ESL students, the following tip may help. When introducting a noun for the first time in your speaking or writing, use an indefinite article. Once this noun has been introduced, it becomes specific, and is then referred to by the definite article.

(I have <u>a</u> fluorescent toothbrush. When the lights are out at night, <u>the</u> toothbrush glows brightly.)

Have a GO! Ans p.105

Fill in the blanks in these sentences:

1 I need ______ pen so that I can fill out ______ form for pottery lessons.

2 Sara always eats ______ orange for breakfast.

3 If Liam enters ______ skateboard competition, I'm sure he'll win ______ trophy.

4 ______ nurses who work in ______ hospital over ______ road wear blue uniforms to distinguish themselves from ______ nurses who work in ______ hospital around ______ corner.

5 I came up with ______ idea and then I wrote it down.

6 You should bring ______ hat and ______ umbrella to the beach, as it will be very sunny.

7 Ray had ______ egg for breakfast, ______ salad for lunch and ______ pizza for tea.

No article

Sometimes, no articles are used at all, especially when the person or thing referred to is **very general**. Plurals often have no articles, especially when used in the general sense.

Look at the examples below to see how general the people or things referred to actually are.

1 People usually eat too much at Christmas time.
2 Children should get plenty of sleep in order to be healthy.
3 George loves vegetables but Meg hates them.
4 Dentists say that apples and milk are good for you.
5 We often eat soup in winter.
6 Doctors need to be able to listen carefully to their patients.
7 We will need scissors, pins, needle and thread to sew this dress.
8 Felt-tipped pens have nice, bright colours.
9 Fruit is good for you.
10 The solar system contains planets, asteroids and comets.

Have a GO! Ans p.105

Fill in the blanks below with definite, indefinite or no articles:

1 I love ___ potatoes with ___ cheese on them.

2 ___ hot potato burnt his mouth.

3 Lena had ___ potato for dinner.

4 ___ students should wear ___ neat uniform to ___ school, to show respect for themselves and their school.

5 I hate ___ spinach but I love ___ carrots.

6 All mammals have ___ hair on their bodies.

7 Diane came top of ___ class.

8 Josh lent ___ sharpener to Tim, but he didn't give it back.

9 ___ Italians and ___ Spaniards love to stay up late.

10 I will give you ___ headache pill, if your headache hasn't gone away after you've had ___ rest.

11 Subjects, predicates and objects

Subjects and predicates

What are they?

Sentences consist of a subject and a predicate.

- The **subject** is the part of the sentence about which a statement is made or a question asked. To find the subject, find the verb in the sentence and ask who or what took part in the action. The answer to this question is the subject.
- The rest of the sentence is the **predicate**.

Examples of subjects and predicates are:

<u>Gina</u> *baked* a cake.

Ask: Who baked the cake? The answer is Gina. 'Gina' is the subject and 'baked a cake' is the predicate.

The car *was damaged* by the hailstorm.

Ask: What was damaged? The answer is 'the car'. 'The car' is the subject and 'was damaged by the hailstorm' is the predicate.

Commands

With a command, the order is being directed at 'you'. Although 'you' isn't mentioned, it is understood.

<u>Go</u> and <u>get</u> your raincoat.

The subject is 'you' (understood), and the predicate is 'go and get your raincoat'.

Have a GO! Ans p.105

See if you can find the subjects and predicates in the following sentences.
Circle the subject and underline the predicate.

1 Jack and Jill ran up the hill.

2 Steven and Sandy live in Killara.

3 Paola watches television in the afternoons.

4 Because of the bad storm, we decided to stay home.

5 The old tramp used to sleep under this bridge.

6 Tanya and Nick go to the city every week.

7 Tomcats often fight at night.

8 How did young Helen break her arm?

9 Please bring me a can of oil.

10 Suddenly, the speeding driver lost control and went over the cliff.

Objects

What are they?

Objects of verbs

Just as a subject tells who or what did the action of a sentence, an object tells what the **action was done to**. To find the object in a sentence, find the verb and then ask to whom or what the action was done.

If the verb has an object, the answer to this question should be a noun or pronoun (or sometimes a noun phrase or clause, as shown in Chapter 14).

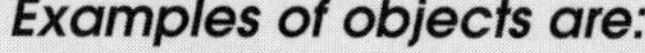

Examples of objects are:

Tom *drank* the milk.

Ask: Drank what? Answer: Milk. Therefore 'milk' is the object of the verb 'drank' in this sentence.

Jack *chased* Daniel around the playground.

Ask: Chased whom? Answer: Daniel. Thus, 'Daniel' is the object of 'chased'.

Objects of prepositions

Objects also come after prepositions. The **noun or pronoun that follows a preposition** is its object. Again, you can ask 'what?' after the preposition and the answer will be the object of that preposition.

Zoe slid *down* the slippery dip.

Ask: Down what? Answer: Slippery dip. Therefore, 'slippery dip' is the object of the preposition 'down'.

Notice in the above sentence, if you ask whom or what of the verb 'slid', as in 'Zoe slid what?', the question doesn't make sense and there is no noun or pronoun answer. The verb 'slid' doesn't have an object in this sentence.

Have a GO! **Ans p.105**

See if you can spot the objects in the following sentences. Underline each object and circle the verb or preposition to which it belongs. Some sentences may contain more than one object, so be careful. For example: Sarah (read) a book (under) a shady tree.

1 Jack's mother told him to sell the cow.

2 Jack sold the cow for magic beans instead of money.

3 The angry mother sent her son to bed in disgrace.

4 Jack threw the magic beans out of the window.

5 In the morning, the boy climbed up the beanstalk.

6 At the top of the beanstalk, Jack discovered a giant's castle in the clouds.

7 The giant owned a hen which laid golden eggs.

12

More about verbs

Simple, continuous and perfect tense

What are they?

As you saw in Chapter 4, verbs have three tenses: the **present**, **past** and **future**. These three tenses also have three styles: the **simple**, the **continuous** and the **perfect**.

As an example, look at the verb 'to run', in the three tenses and three styles of tense:

- run (present simple); ran (past simple); will run (future simple)
- is running (present continuous); was running (past continuous); will be running (future continuous)
- has run (present perfect); had run (past perfect); will have run (future perfect).

Simple tense

The simple tense uses the principal verb to describe the action being done.
This tense is used:

- to show an activity that **happens regularly**
- when using **sense and feeling verbs**: smell, taste, see, hear, understand, feel, know, believe.

We go to the shops on Saturdays.

This tastes horrible!

I know where you live.

Continuous tense

The continuous tense uses the principal verb with the verb 'to be' in front of it. This tense shows that the action **is or was in progress**.

I am eating my dinner.

She was running to school when the lightning struck.

Perfect tense

The perfect tense uses the principal verb with the verb 'to have' in front of it.

The **present perfect** tense shows that the action **began in the past and is continuing into the present.** Compare the meanings of the following examples:

I have lived in Brisbane for two years. (and still do: present perfect)

I lived in Brisbane for two years. (but don't anymore: past simple)

The **past perfect** tense indicates an action that happened **in the past before another action took place.**

The snow had fallen all day, before they closed the roads.

In April, they repaired the streets, which had cracked during the earthquake.

Auxiliary verbs

What are they?

The words such as 'will', 'has', 'had', 'will be' and 'will have' that come **before the principal verb** are called auxiliary verbs. Their job is to help put the principal verb into the future, continuous or perfect tense.

There are also other types of auxiliary verbs: can, could, would, should, might, must, ought and may.

Have a GO! Ans p.105

In the following exercise, see if you can state the **tense** and **style of tense** being used. For example: I go to the shops every Monday. (present, simple)

1 Maryam is reading a book. ____________________

2 Stephen went to the Royal Easter Show. ____________________

3 Gloria has eaten her lunch. ____________________

4 Grace was crying in the bath. ____________________

5 Meg believes in ghosts. ____________________

6 Tina will come to the cinema with us. ____________________

7 Tsugu had gone before I arrived. ____________________

8 Bryn will have read his book by now. ____________________

9 I will be walking in the bush next week. ____________________

10 Benn skates to school. ____________________

11 Adam wears trendy clothes. ____________________

12 Andrew wore Alan's old clothes. ____________________

13 Kay will get a new dress at the markets. ____________________

14 Richard spilt tomato sauce all over his T-shirt. ____________________

15 Sandy has been skating at the ice rink. ____________________

Finite and non-finite verbs

What are they?

Verbs can be finite (**having a subject**) or non-finite (**having no subject**).

Finite verbs

Finite verbs have a subject.
A sentence must have a finite verb, in order for it to make sense. Finite verbs can be simple or accompanied by an auxiliary verb.

The tree crashed to the ground.

Ask: What crashed? The tree crashed. 'Tree' is the subject of the verb 'crashed'. Therefore, 'crashed' is a finite verb. ('Crashed' is a simple finite verb, standing alone without the need of an auxiliary verb).

Graham is going to the Blue Mountains.

Who is going? Graham is. 'Graham' is the subject of the verb 'is going' and therefore 'is going' is finite. ('Going' by itself is non-finite. It needs the help of the auxiliary verb 'is' to make it finite.)

Non-finite verbs

Non-finite verbs do not have a subject. If you ask who or what did the action, you will get no answer.

There are two types of non-finite verbs: the infinitive and the participle.

1 **The infinitive**. This is the verb without any connection to a subject. Infinitives usually have a 'to' in front of them: to run, to jump, to be, to have, to go.

   It is not the right time to go to the shops.

   Ask: Who or what to go? There is no answer because there is no subject, and therefore the infinitive 'to go' is non-finite.

2 **The participle**. There are two types: present participles, which end in 'ing', and past participles, which end in 'ed' or 'en' or have irregular forms. Unless participles are accompanied by an auxiliary verb, they have no subject and are non-finite.

   Examples of **present participles** are:

   Walking blindfolded across the room, I tripped over the carpet.

   Ask: Who walking? This doesn't make sense and has no subject. 'Walking' is non-finite.

Slinking quietly into his room, the teenager hoped his parents wouldn't realise how late home he was.

Ask: Who slinking? No answer. 'Slinking' is non-finite.

Examples of **past participles** are:

Written on the wall in big letters was a sign saying 'No Trespassers!'

The car was a wreck, crushed by a falling boulder.

If you ask who or what did the action with these past participle verbs, you will find there is no subject and the verbs are non-finite.

Have a GO! **Ans p.105**

Circle all the finite verbs in the following sentences, and **underline** all the non-finite ones. If they are non-finite, write 'inf' for infinitive, 'pres' for a present participle or 'past' for a past participle underneath the word.

1 The teacher told the naughty boy to go to the principal's office.

____

2 Clapping their hands loudly, the people rose to their feet.

____

3 Chained to the wall, the convict could barely move.

____

4 Ken was playing Nintendo for four hours.

____

5 Anne had ridden her bike to the shops, without telling her mum.

____

Transitive and intransitive verbs

What are they?

Transitive verbs have **an object**.

An example of a transitive verb is:

I ate an egg for breakfast.

Ask: I ate what? An egg. 'Egg' is the object of the verb 'ate' and therefore 'ate' is a transitive verb.

Intransitive verbs don't have an object.

An example of an intransitive verb is:

The baby crawled around the bedroom.

Ask: The baby crawled what? There is no answer and no object of the verb 'crawled'. 'Crawled' is therefore an intransitive verb.

Have a GO! Ans p.105

Say whether the underlined verbs in the following sentences are transitive or intransitive. If they are transitive, put the object in brackets. For example: Lynn likes peaches and mangoes. Transitive (peaches and mangoes).

1 The engineers built a bridge across the river. ____________________

2 The Romans loved hot baths. ____________________

3 Charlie likes to play with Rover. ____________________

4 The noisy teenagers stormed into the house. ____________________

5 We read the sad news in the paper. ____________________

6 We read until late at night. ____________________

7 Kerry won the three-legged race at school. ____________________

8 He won easily. ____________________

9 Ned loves cars but Kosta doesn't. ____________________

10 The witch flew away on her broomstick. ____________________

13

Gerunds

What are they?

Gerunds are verbal nouns. They are **the names of actions** and look like verbs but act like nouns. They always end in 'ing'. As with nouns, the possessive case comes before a gerund if it belongs to someone, as can be seen in sentences 4 and 6.

Examples of gerunds are:

1 You need nimble fingers to do sewing and knitting.

2 Shouting is not allowed in the library.

3 This endless talking will just have to stop.

4 Your studying of German will help you when you travel.

5 Swearing is ugly and undignified.

6 John's learning of karate has stopped the bullies from pestering him.

7 The landing of men on the moon was a great event in our history.

8 Listening is as important as writing when it comes to learning.

9 Staring at that man is rude behaviour.

Don't confuse gerunds with present participle verbs, which also end in 'ing'. To test for gerunds, say 'the action of' before the gerund. If it makes sense, the word is a gerund and not a present participle.

Have a GO! Ans p.105

Underline the gerunds in the sentences below:

1 Cheating will get you nowhere.

2 Michael's shouting drives people mad.

3 Knowing how to swim could save your life.

4 A love of reading helps you become knowledgeable.

5 I am reading the writing in Simon's workbook.

In the following sentences underline the gerunds and circle the present participles.

6 We are going out after doing the laundry.

7 Toko has been living in the Blue Mountains ever since buying a house up there.

8 Most people are shy of speaking in public, fearing criticism from the audience.

9 Hiking is a healthy pastime. I am going hiking this weekend.

14

Phrases

What are they?

Phrases are little groups of words in a sentence **without a finite verb**.

Examples of phrases are:

- **Prepositional** phrases start with a preposition. For example:

  Jack fell down the hill.

- **Participial** phrases start with present or past participles. For example:

  Jumping for joy, the two children ran through the gates of the Royal Easter Show.
  The town was in ruins, destroyed by the violent tornado.

- **Infinitive** phrases start with infinitives. For example:

  To play the game well, you will need to practise a lot.

- **Gerund** phrases start with gerunds. For example: Knowing your multiplication tables well is the doorway to more advanced maths.

Ans p.106

Look at the sentences below and try to spot the phrases. Underline them and state whether they begin with a preposition, a participle, an infinitive or a gerund.

1 We hid under the house, so they wouldn't see us. ____________________

2 The cow jumped over the moon. ____________________

3 Cackling with laughter, the witch sped away on her broomstick. ____________________

4 To be late is better than not to come at all. ____________________

5 Written in red ink, the magic spell was there for all to see. ____________________

6 Hidden somewhere among the crowd, a time-bomb was ticking away.

____

GO!

7 When Newton was sitting under a tree, an apple dropped on his head.

____

8 Writing neatly will give you higher marks in your assignment.

____

9 I think that riding on the Rotor at Luna Park is very scary. _______________

Phrase types

Phrases can act as adjectives, adverbs or nouns.

- If a phrase **describes a noun**, it is called an **adjectival phrase**.
- If the phrase **describes a verb**, it is called an **adverbial phrase**.
- If the phrase **acts like a noun**, it is called a **noun phrase**. Noun phrases can act as either the subject or the object of a sentence. They usually begin with infinitive or gerund phrases.

Here are some examples:

The man with the brown hat is my uncle.

This phrase describes the man, so it is an adjectival phrase.

The tightrope walker balanced on his tip-toes.

This phrase describes how the balancing was done, so it is an adverbial phrase (of manner).

To argue with the teacher was asking for trouble.

This phrase acts like a noun and is a noun phrase. (A noun phrase can be checked by substituting the word 'something' in its place, and the sentence will still make sense).

By learning to use phrases well, you will add variety to your compositions.

Have a GO! **Ans p.106**

Underline all the phrases in the following sentences, and state whether they are adjectival, adverbial or noun phrases.

1 The mice in the cage are very active. _______________

2 Edwina ran in great terror from the fire-breathing dragon. _______________

3 Walking through the park at night is risky. _______________

4 The black swans slept among the reeds. _______________

5 Tired out after the long trip, he went straight to sleep. _______________

6 Building the dam provided plenty of water for the farmers' crops. _______________

7 To sleepwalk is a strange thing to do. _______________

8 Many knights tried to pull the sword from the stone. _______________

9 Outside the village, Philip met a man with a long, grey beard.

____

10 The axe used by the criminal was found in the cellar, covered with blood.

____

15

Person

What is it?

Person refers to the direction of the sentence:

- **First person** sentences are **spoken by the speaker**, using the pronouns 'I' for singular and 'we' for plural.
- **Second person** sentences are **spoken to the listener**, using the pronoun 'you' (singular or plural).
- **Third person** sentences are **spoken about someone else**, using 'he', 'she' or 'it' in the singular and 'they' in the plural. The third person can also be shown by the use of people's names, showing that they are spoken about.

Examples of person are:

I will live on an island, when I get rich. (first person, singular)

You had better tidy your bag, Jo, before you go to school. (second person, singular)

He broke his leg, when he fell off his bike. (third person, singular)

We shall go to the beach when everybody is ready. (first person, plural)

You children must do your homework before it gets dark. (second person, plural)

They went in a helicopter to see what it was like. (third person, plural)

Hans is the cleverest boy in the class. (third person, singular)

Duncan and Tom are brothers. (third person, plural)

Have a GO! Ans p.106

State the person and number of the following sentences.

1 Get out of my house, with your muddy feet! ____________________

2 She is so lazy, she will never do well at school. ____________________

3 It was the most beautiful sunset that I had ever seen. ____________________

4 They have travelled all over the world and like Switzerland most of all. ____________________

5 You girls will get cold, if you don't put on your jumpers. ____________________

6 We went on a picnic yesterday and a big bull chased us across the field. ____________________

7 He is a bully at school and nobody likes him. ____________________

8 Jessica and Steven brought their new puppy to school. ____________________

9 Tina is in Year 7 and she catches the bus to school. ____________________

10 Daniel and his baby sister were both born in Melbourne. ____________________

11 I was very scared when I looked around the haunted house. ____________________

12 Paul and I have known each other for many years. ____________________

13 You two should go into the mirror maze and see if you can find your way out. ____________________

16

Case

What is it?

There are three cases in English: **subjective**, **objective** and **possessive**.

Subjective case

Subjective (nominative) case is for nouns and pronouns in the **subject** of the sentence.

Joel missed the school bus because he slept in.

Who missed the bus? Joel did. 'Joel' is the subject of the sentence and is in the subjective case.

We climbed the mountain for a beautiful view of the landscape.

Who climbed the mountain? We did. 'We' is the subject of the sentence and is in the subjective case.

'To be'

The verb 'to be' takes the subjective case both **before and after** it.

It is I who was knocking on the door.

'I' follows the verb 'is' (which is part of the verb 'to be') and is in the subjective case.

Objective case

Objective (accusative) case is for nouns and pronouns that are the **object** of a sentence. Both verbs and prepositions can form the objective case.

Please *give* the book *to* John tomorrow.

Give what? Give the book. 'Book' is the object of the verb 'give' and is in the objective case.

Give the book to whom? To John. 'John' is the object of the preposition 'to' and is also in the objective case.

Wendy hit me accidentally.

Hit whom? Hit me. 'Me' is the object of the verb 'hit' and is in the objective case.

Jack and Jill went up the hill.

Went up what? Up the hill. 'Hill' is the object of the preposition 'up' and is in the objective case.

Possessive case

Possessive (genitive) case is for nouns and pronouns that show **possession** or ownership of something.

Mark's exam results were excellent.

The exam results belong to Mark, as shown by the apostrophe. 'Mark's' is in the possessive case.

His thinking is illogical and he should be more rational.

The thinking belongs to him, and 'his' is in the possessive case.

This bag is mine and that one over there is yours.

The bags belong to me and you, so 'mine' and 'yours' are in the possessive case.

Declension of pronouns

Pronouns are declined to show case, person, number and gender.

Person and number	Subjective	Objective	Possessive
First singular	I	me	mine
Second singular	you	you	yours
Third singular	he	him	his
Third singular	she	her	hers
Third singular	it	it	its
First plural	we	us	ours
Second plural	you	you	yours
Third plural	they	them	theirs
Third singular and plural	who	whom	whose

Ans p.106

State the case of the underlined words in the following sentences.

1 Emily helped Mike with his homework because hers was already finished.

2 Tsugu gave a mango to Yoshi, as it is Yoshi's favourite fruit.

3 I don't like you one single bit! You are an unfriendly and selfish person.

4 The balloon crashed to the ground. Everyone survived, but the balloon was a wreck.

5 It was we who were hiding behind the tree. We tricked you, and we know your secret.

17

Converting to another part of speech

What is it?

In your writing and speaking, when trying to find the correct word to use, you will sometimes find it handy to be able to convert from one part of speech into another.

An example of conversion is:

Emily was in danger. (noun)
Emily was endangered. (verb)

Common suffixes for the main parts of speech:

Nouns often end in: *-ment, -ledge, -hood, -dom, -ty, -y, -ness, -ery, -ary, -ory.*

Verbs often end in: *-ise, -en, -ify.*
Sometimes they also begin with *en-.*

Adjectives *often end in: -ous, -ful, -ic, -ing, -less, -able, -ible, -ed, -ive.*

Adverbs often end in: *-ly, -ally.*

Have a GO! Ans p.106

Fill in the following table, transforming the words given into the four main parts of speech. One or two of the words might not be able to be converted to all four parts of speech.

Noun	Verb	Adjective	Adverb
		large	
danger			
energy			
	enjoy		
	talk		
		beautiful	
		empty	
	embarrass		
			speedily
			bravely
		quiet	
peace			
	hate		
		fantastic	
horror			
	study		
		glorious	
life			
	know		

18

Voice and mood

Voice

What is it?

The voice of a verb tells whether the subject **does the action** or whether something is **done to it**. There are two voices: **active** and **passive**.

Active voice

In the active voice, **the subject does the action** of the verb.

Zeb climbed the wall.

The verb 'climbed' is in the active voice because the subject 'Zeb' is doing the climbing.

Passive voice

In the passive voice, **the subject is inactive** and an action is done to it. The verb used in the passive voice consists of an auxiliary verb with the past participle.

The fence was climbed by Zeb.

'The fence' is the subject and it is inactive. The 'climbing' is done to it.

Have a GO! Ans p.107

Say whether the following sentences are in the active or passive voice.

1 I burnt my hand on the hotplate. ______

2 The space station was put into orbit by NASA. ______

3 Jane's broken arm was put into plaster by the doctor. ______

4 The speeding driver crashed into the telegraph pole and cracked his skull open. ______

5 Your knowledge of geography will be tested at the next exams. ______

6 Monty, the labrador, thinks the park is the best place on Earth. ______

Mood

What is it?

There are four moods that a verb can take in English. These are the **indicative**, **interrogative**, **imperative** and **subjunctive**.

Indicative mood

The indicative mood is used for **statements** and **exclamations**.

The butcher worked very long hours. (statement)

Thank Heavens you're safe! (exclamation)

Interrogative mood

The interrogative mood is used for **questions**.

How old will you be in June?

Imperative mood

The imperative mood is used for **commands** and **giving orders**.

Clean your bedroom up at once.

Please bring me a cup of tea.

Do your homework before you go out.

Subjunctive mood

The subjunctive mood is used to express a **wish**, an **impossibility**, a **necessity** or an **uncertainty**. These conditions are expressed after words like these: if, wish, that, as though, as if.

If I <u>were</u> you, I wouldn't do that. (impossibility)

I wish he <u>were</u> with us right now. (wish)

The police insisted that he <u>tell</u> the whole story. (necessity)

She looked as though she were completely lost. (uncertainty)

If you are coming with us, it is essential that you be here early. (necessity)

The white figure moved smoothly past, as if it were a ghost. (uncertainty)

The conjugation of verbs in the subjunctive mood is different from usual.

- The 's' ending in the third person singular is dropped (e.g. I look, you look, he look).
- The verb 'to be' is simply 'be' in all persons in the present tense (e.g. I be, you be, he be) and 'were' in all persons in the past tense (e.g. I were, you were, he were).

Have a GO! Ans p.107

See if you can state the mood of each of these sentences.

1 My favourite time of year is autumn. ____________________

2 How do you get to Kakadu from Darwin? ____________________

3 God save the Queen. ____________________

4 I wish that he be kept safe from harm, while he is travelling. ____________________

5 Go to your room this minute. ____________________

6 Robbie is being home-schooled for a few years. ____________________

7 I vote that she be invested as a Cub Scout next Monday. ____________________

8 Good grief! Look at the time! ____________________

9 Did you find the film scary? ____________________

10 If I were a millionaire, I would give a lot of money to charity. ____________________

11 The teacher insists that he come for an afternoon detention. ____________________

12 Bring in the washing before it rains, please Becky. ____________________

13 The old woman next door dresses as if she were a teenager. ____________________

14 She ran as if she were an Olympian. ____________________

15 It is essential that I be at the station by 7 o'clock. ____________________

19

Clauses

What are they?

A clause is a group of words containing **a finite verb**. There are several different types of clauses which have different functions within a sentence.

Principal and subordinate clauses

- If the clause makes sense on its own, it is called a **principal clause**.
- If the clause doesn't make sense by itself, it is called a **subordinate clause**.

Children like toys.

This group of words contains the finite verb 'like' and it makes sense on its own. Therefore it is a principal clause.

We had to go home, because it was pouring with rain.

The first part of the sentence (We had to go home) makes sense alone, but the second part (because it was pouring with rain) can't stand on its own. It needs the help of the principal clause to make sense. It is subordinate to the principal clause and tells a bit more about the principal clause.

I ran quickly but I didn't win.

Sometimes sentences have two principal clauses joined by a conjunction. Here they are joined by 'but'.

The number of finite verbs in a sentence equals the number of clauses. A sentence with only one clause is a **simple sentence**. A sentence with a principal and a subordinate clause is a **complex sentence**, and a sentence with two principal clauses is a **compound sentence**.

Have a GO! Ans p.107

Pick out the principal and subordinate clauses below. Underline the **principal** clauses and circle the **subordinate** clauses.

1 I saw you when you hid behind that tree.

2 That is the girl who came top of the class.

3 We all know that it is your birthday tomorrow.

4 Andy and Rachel always have dinner after they have had a bath.

5 We were very sad when those poor men died in the submarine.

6 William asked for pavlova, because it is his favourite dessert.

7 Tadpoles live in the water and frogs live on the land.

8 This is my pet rat, which sleeps in my slipper.

9 While watching the long game of cricket, I fell asleep.

10 This is the house where I was born.

11 You take the high road and I'll take the low road.

12 Be thankful that you are fit and healthy.

Adjectival clauses

If the subordinate clause **describes the noun** in the principal clause, it acts like an adjective and is called an adjectival clause.

This is the cat that killed the poor sparrow.

'That killed the poor sparrow' is an adjectival clause describing the cat.

Adverbial clauses

If the subordinate clause tells more **about the verb** in the principal clause, it acts like an adverb and is called an adverbial clause.

- Just as adverbs can tell 'how' (**manner**), 'when' (**time**) or 'where' (**place**) about a verb, so can adverbial clauses.
- They can also tell 'why' about the verb and are called adverbial clauses of **reason**.
- Adverbial clauses can also tell about **condition** (if, unless), **purpose** (so that, in order that), **result** (that, so that), **comparison** (than, as much as, just as) and **concession** (though, although), but we will just concentrate on time, manner, place and reason.

We will come home when we are ready.

'When we are ready' is an adverbial clause of time, telling **when** we will come.

Mark failed his test because he didn't study.

'Because he didn't study' is an adverbial clause of reason, telling **why** he failed.

The children hid where no one could see them.

'Where no one could see them' is an adverbial clause of place, telling **where** they hid.

The boys gobbled down their dinner as if they were starving.

'As if they were starving' is an adverbial clause of manner, telling **how** the boys gobbled.

Noun clauses

If a subordinate clause **behaves like a noun**, it is called a noun clause. Just as nouns do, a noun clause can act as the subject or object of a verb. An easy way to detect a noun clause is to substitute the word 'something' in its place, and if this makes sense, then the clause is a noun clause. Noun clauses often begin with 'that'.

I thought I told you that you should go to bed early.

I thought I told you 'something' makes sense, so 'that you should go to bed early' is a noun clause.

Have a GO! Ans p.107

Try your best to state what type of subordinate clauses the underlined words are:

1 Jim knows where the stream goes.

____

2 The passenger train that I went on has a sleeping and dining car.

____

3 We went to church because it was Christmas.

____

4 Everyone says that you should wear sun cream and a hat.

____

5 What they saw in the haunted house is a mystery.

____

6 The snow, which fell last night, is thick and beautiful.

____

7 The girls swim where there are no dangerous currents.

____

8 Brett built the model as though he were an engineer.

____

9 The Scouts went camping just before the blizzard began.

____

20

Sentences

Courteous order

What is it?

In traditional grammar, it is considered correct and polite, when speaking or writing about yourself and others, that you **mention yourself last**.

Correct: John, Jackie and I went to the beach this morning.

Incorrect: Me, John and Jackie went to the beach today.

Correct: The cake was shared between Graham and me.

Incorrect: The cake was shared between me and Graham.

In the incorrect first example, apart from the fact that courteous order has not been used, 'me' is wrong because it is in the subject of the sentence and should therefore be 'I'. In the second example, the use of 'me' is correct, because it is in the objective case, but courteous order has not been followed.

Sentence types

A sentence is a group of words that **makes sense,** has a **subject** and a **finite verb**.

The man climbed the mountain.

This group of words has a verb (climbed) with a subject (the man), makes sense and therefore is a sentence.

Climbing the stairs, the boy

This group of words has a verb (climbing), but no subject (is non-finite) and it doesn't make sense, so it is not a sentence.

Have a GO! **Ans p.108**

Tick which of the following are sentences, and put a cross against those that are not:

1 Nicholas is only six.

2 Jumping through the hoop, the lion.

3 Looking through the door, she saw the burglar climb out of the window.

4 When we were away.

5 Ruined by the earthquake.

6 James cried.

7 Crying like a baby.

8 Ninety-two people with hats.

9 Ninety-two people have hats.

Types of sentences

Sentences come in four varieties:

1 **statements,** which state facts

2 **questions,** which ask something

3 **commands,** which order something to be done

4 **exclamations,** which say something with surprise or strong feeling.

Here are some examples:

Jill has blonde hair. (statement)

It rained yesterday. (statement)

Have you finished your homework? (question)

What an exciting film that was! (exclamation)

Please make me a cup of coffee. (command)

Don't forget to mow the lawn before you go out. (command)

Oh, no! We're late! (exclamation)

Have a GO! **Ans p.108**

After each sentence write whether the sentence is a statement, question, command or exclamation.

1 Is Tony coming home today? ____________________

2 Tony is coming home today. ____________________

3 Come home today, Tony. ____________________

4 Hooray! Tony's come home today! ____________________

5 Get into that bath at once, you muddy boy. ____________________

6 Do you like grammar? ____________________

7 Oh, my golly gosh! ______________________________

8 Ouch! That hurt! ______________________________

9 Most people like grammar. ______________________________

10 Get the mail and see if Adam has sent us a postcard. ______________________________

Simple, complex and compound sentences

As mentioned in 'Clauses', sentences can be **simple** (one principal clause), **complex** (a principal and subordinate clause), or **compound** (two principal clauses joined by a conjunction).

For example: I love peaches. (simple sentence)
I love peaches because they're sweet. (complex sentence)
I love peaches but Jack loves mangoes. (compound sentence)

Parsing and analysis

What are they?

Once you can **parse and analyse a sentence correctly**, you can truly say that you have mastered the art of grammar. Parsing and analysis are the true tests of your grammatical knowledge and understanding.

Parsing

Parsing involves looking at each word in a sentence and then:

1 stating to what part of speech the word belongs;

2 describing its form (person, number, mood, voice, tense, etc.);

3 explaining its relationship to other words in the same sentence.

Look at this example:

Craig won the cross-country race with ease.

Craig — noun: proper, singular, masculine, subjective case, subject of 'won'
won — verb: past simple tense, third person, singular, finite (subject = Craig), transitive (object = race), irregular conjugation, indicative mood, active voice
the — definite article qualifying 'race'
cross-country — adjective, descriptive, qualifying 'race'
race — noun, abstract, singular, neuter, objective case, object of 'won'
with — preposition governing 'ease'
ease — noun, abstract, singular, neuter, objective case, object of 'with'.

Have a GO! Ans p.107

Try to parse the sentences below:

1 We have a dog and two guinea pigs.

2 Action films are spectacular to watch.

Analysis

Analysis involves breaking a sentence into its functional parts:

- In simple sentences with only one finite verb, **subject and predicate** are examined, with subject, verb, object and descriptive words or phrases (adjectives and adverbs) analysed.
- In longer sentences with two or more finite verbs, **principal and subordinate clauses** are examined, with subordinate clauses being analysed for their type and their relationship to the principal clause.

Look at this simple sentence:

All the children in Year 7 will get an early mark this afternoon.

Subject: 'All the children in Year 7'. The noun in the subject is 'children', the adjective qualifying 'children' is 'all' and the adjectival phrase qualifying 'children' is 'in Year 7'.

Predicate: 'will get an early mark this afternoon'. The verb in the predicate is 'will get', the object of the verb is 'early mark' and the adverbial phrase of time modifying 'will get' is 'this afternoon'.

Here is a complex sentence:

> Trudy and Thao, who are best of friends, go to Guides after they have done their homework.

Principal clause: Trudy and Thao go to Guides

Subordinate clause 1: who are best of friends (adjectival clause qualifying 'Trudy and Thao')

Subordinate clause 2: after they have done their homework (adverbial clause of time, modifying 'go')

Have a GO! **Ans p.107**

Have a go at analysing these sentences:

1 We went to the Sushi Train for lunch, because we had heard how good it was.

2 In summer, Oki went to the Outback and Kathi visited Tasmania.

21 Punctuation

Basic punctuation

What is it?

Punctuation helps you understand the meaning of a sentence.

- All sentences start with a **capital letter**.
- Statements and commands end with a **full stop**.
- Questions end with a **question mark** (?).
- Exclamations end with an **exclamation mark** (!).

Have a GO! Ans p.108

Decide what type of sentences the following are and then punctuate them correctly, using capitals, full stops, question marks and exclamation marks. (Remember that proper nouns also start with capital letters.)

1 we went to the zoo on saturday

____

____

2 have you been to the zoo recently

____

____

3 what a disgusting mess

____

____

4 peel the potatoes while i bath the baby

5 how old will you be this year

6 do you own a ford or a holden

7 please make your bed before breakfast

8 have you made your bed yet

9 what a helpful girl you are

10 good children help their parents around the home

11 whats your favourite song

12 play the piano for us

13 do you know how to play the violin

14 most korean children learn to play an instrument

15 well done you clever girl

Have a GO! Ans p.108

See if you can punctuate the following paragraph:

when i was a teenager the men landed on the moon for the first time and it was so exciting i was at school and we watched the men get out of their rocket we were scared that the moon dust might be very soft and that the men might sink right under the surface luckily that didn't happen the men walked around collecting moon rocks and putting them in a bag so that they could be studied back on earth because gravity is less on the moon than on earth the men could jump very high even with their heavy spacesuits on would you like to go to the moon one day I would

Commas

What are they?

You already know when to use full stops, question marks and exclamation marks. Now you need to learn about the correct use of commas. Commas are used when **a pause is needed** in a sentence, to help it make sense.

Rule 1

Use commas **between two or more nouns, verbs, prepositions or adjectives.**

I bought bread, milk, butter and cheese.

At Little Athletics we run, hurdle, jump, walk and throw.

We looked on, under, behind and inside the desk, but we still couldn't find it.

It was a dark, cold, windy night.

Rule 2

If a sentence starts with a conjunction, place a comma at the join **between the two clauses.**

Unless you do your homework, you won't be going out tonight.

Rule 3

If a sentence is long or complex, and would be made clearer by the use of a pause or pauses, then use a comma **where a pause is needed.**

I've just read a physics book about Superstring Theory, but I found it so complicated, and my maths just wasn't good enough to grasp the concepts, so I still don't understand Superstrings, much to my sorrow.

Rule 4

If there is an interruption or change of thought in the sentence, use a comma to **show the change of flow.**

No, I didn't say that.

Come to think of it, I do dream in colour.

By the way, the postman delivered this letter.

Uranus, however, is different from the other planets.

Rule 5

If someone is spoken to directly, using their name, use commas to **separate the name from the rest of the sentence.**

Harry, come here at once.

You, William, have been very disobedient.

Rule 6

If the sentence starts with an adjectival or adverbial phrase, use a comma **after the phrase.**

Veiled by the mist, the mountains looked eerie. (adjectival phrase)

In the morning, we go for a surf before breakfast. (adverbial phrase of time)

Way up in Iceland, the winter days are dark and cold. (adverbial phrase of place)

Because of the wet weather, we came home early. (adverbial phrase of reason)

With fear in his eyes, the boy saw the ghost step into the mirror. (adverbial phrase of manner)

Rule 7

If a sentence contains a group of words that adds **detail that isn't essential**, put commas around these words.

Robert, my brother, is a school teacher.

At midnight, while I was asleep, it started to snow.

The Olympic gymnastics, which were held in the Superdome, were just fantastic.

Rule 8

If quotation marks are used to show speech, put a comma just **before the quotation marks** (or just after the quotation, if it begins the sentence).

The Goblin said to the Hobbit, ' Take me to the Pixies or I will tell the Dragon.'

'I won first prize in the yo-yo competition,' Ramu told his parents proudly.

Notice, also, that the first letter of a quotation should be spelt with a capital letter.

Have a GO! **Ans p.108**

To practise the above rules, see if you can put commas in the correct places in the following sentences.

1. We bought apples pears bananas and oranges for the fruit salad.
2. The dinosaur was a long-toothed sharp-clawed quick-footed bloodthirsty vicious monster.
3. Although we arrived early the restaurant was full.
4. Diana clean the duck's cage before you come inside.
5. Yes you can put the Christmas tree up tomorrow.
6. My two sons who like to stay up late are always tired in the morning.
7. The magician did some magic tricks with a rabbit and a pack of cards and then the acrobats went on the flying trapeze.
8. Believe it or not I saw a pig fly past the window.
9. If you eat your vegetables you may have dessert.
10. Lizards snakes tortoises and turtles are all reptiles.
11. Sean you must tell the truth.
12. The boys even the tall ones were short compared with the basketball players.
13. I said no but they came anyway.
14. If life is here on Earth couldn't it be on other planets as well?
15. I think Rugby League players are great big stupid oafs!
16. To be honest with you I really don't know.
17. The teacher said 'Do your homework by Friday.'
18. 'Get out of my room at once' shouted Julia angrily.
19. Creeping quietly down the hall the girl saw Father Christmas unloading presents.
20. Late at night we sometimes look at the stars through our telescope.

Have a GO! Ans p.109

Punctuate the following, being careful with punctuation around any quotations:

what was armstrongs pulse rate when he set foot on the moon i asked oh surprisingly it was much lower than when he was landing in his rocket answered the nasa expert the problem was that he was low on fuel so low in fact that if he hadnt landed when he did he would have crashed good grief i replied they never told us that well he had only five seconds of fuel left and his pulse rate was racing as you can well imagine explained the man from nasa

Quotation marks

What are they?

Quotation marks can also be called 'inverted commas'. They are used in three different ways:

- to quote the **name** of a written work, film or poem
- to **highlight a particular word** to show a different level of usage
- to quote **direct speech**.

Names of written works, films or poems

The names of written works, films or newspapers, when written by hand, are surrounded by quotation marks.

1 I saw 'Speed' at the cinema yesterday. (film)

2 Have you read 'A Tale of Two Cities'? (book)

3 My mum always buys the 'Sydney Morning Herald'. (newspaper)

4 'Hamlet' is one of Shakespeare's best known plays. (play)

5 'The Raven' is a very famous poem by Edgar Allen Poe. (poem)

When you are using a computer, you can use italics in place of the quotation marks for these occasions, just as you will see in published books.

Highlighting particular words

When writing formally, quotation marks are used to highlight particular words to show a different level of usage, including unfamiliar technical words, slang and colloquial words, and words used in a sarcastic manner:

1 The technician who worked in the Microscopy Department told me that she used a 'microtome' for slicing up very thin layers of tissue. (unfamiliar technical word)

2 The recent expedition to Mt Everest, which resulted in the deaths of three mountaineers, was described as a real 'cock-up', being badly organised from the very start. (slang)

3 The foul-mouthed, drunken politician set such a 'fine example' for the young people attending the conference. (sarcasm)

Direct speech

Examples of quotation marks used for direct speech, to quote the exact words used by the speaker are:

1 James cried out to Drew, with fear in his voice, 'Help me, Drew. I'm about to lose my grip.'

2 'When you get up,' asked Wendy's mother, 'please make your bed, and tidy your room.'

Notice in the examples above:

- Commas are used to separate the direct speech from the rest of the sentence.
- The quote begins with a capital letter.
- If a quote is interrupted in the middle of a sentence and is then restarted, the second part of the sentence does not start with a capital.

Other points to note, when using quotation marks around direct speech are:

- **Long quotes**, which cover several paragraphs, start each paragraph with an opening quotation mark, but do not use a closing quotation mark except in the last paragraph of the quote.
- Every **change of speaker** requires a new paragraph with a new set of quotation marks.
- If a quote is used **within another quote**, the internal quote is surrounded by double quotation marks.
- **Commas and full stops** are placed inside the closing quotation marks.
- **Semi-colons and colons** are placed outside the quotation marks.
- **Question and exclamation marks** are placed inside the quotation marks if they are part of the quote, but outside the quotation marks if they relate to the structure of the sentence as a whole.

Have a look at the following examples:

1 Mr Smith stated, in an excited voice, 'I was talking to my stockbroker and he said, "Sell now, sell now!" so I did, and I made an absolute fortune.' (quote within a quote)

2 'Don't go into that house down the road,' warned the old man.
'Why not?' I asked. (change of speaker/punctuation inside quotes)
'It's haunted. Terrible things have happened in there!'
'But I don't believe in ghosts,' I said with great confidence and a smirk on my face.
'Well, you'll believe in ghosts if you go in there and ever make it out alive,' he said.

3 I felt sick when the teacher said to me, 'You've failed'! (exclamation mark outside quote)

4 Did you really believe me when I said, 'I refuse to pay'? (question mark outside quote)

Have a GO! Ans p.109

Do your best to punctuate the following sentences:

1 Edward said I tried my hardest to explain to her what had happened but she yelled get out of my way I never want to see you again so I went home feeling very depressed

2 Which way do we go now screamed Michael how should I know I yelled back I've never been here before I reminded him yes you have screeched Michael in a panicky voice

3 Did you really believe the gypsy when she said I can tell your future

4 I couldn't believe my luck when the man rang me and said you've won the lottery

Other punctuation marks

Less commonly used punctuation marks include colons (:), semi-colons (;) and dashes (-).

Colons

Colons are used before a list of items.

Go to the shops and buy these items for me please: eggs, butter, milk, cheese and apples.

Semi-colons

Semi-colons are used to show a longer pause than a comma but a shorter pause than a full stop. They are normally used to separate two principal clauses which are closely related to each other.

Please close the window; the room is cold.

Dashes

Dashes are used to show a sudden break in thought, an emphasis or an omission of letters or words.

Should we — in fact, could we — alter Mars' environment to be like Earth's?

I was surprised — shocked more like it — to hear the news.

In spans of numbers, your work will look better if you use a short dash or double hyphen:

The 1914–1918 world war is known as World War I.

Apostrophes

What are they?

Apostrophes are used in two ways:

- to show where a letter has been left out in a **contraction**
- to show ownership or **possession**.

Contractions

Contractions are shortened words in which two words have been joined into one, with one or more letters omitted in the join. An apostrophe is used to show the join.

they are	=	they're	shall not	=	shan't
should not	=	shouldn't	she will	=	she'll
cannot	=	can't	will not	=	won't
we have	=	we've	it is	=	it's
he would	=	he'd			

Possession

Possessive nouns have apostrophes to show ownership. Care should be taken to put the apostrophe in its correct position.

Generally, singular possessive nouns use an apostrophe before the 's' and plural possessive nouns use an apostrophe after the 's'.

the dog of the boy = the boy's dog

the dog of the boys = the boys' dog

This simple rule, though, is more difficult than it first seems, and not all plurals have an apostrophe after the 's'. Therefore the following rule will help avoid mistakes with apostrophes.

How to put apostrophes in the right place

Step 1: Convert the possessive noun into the 'French style', so that the owner is separated from the possession by the use of an 'of '.

1 Wendy's dress = the dress of Wendy
2 the river's mouth = the mouth of the river
3 the girls' shoes = the shoes of the girls
4 the children's faces = the faces of the children
5 Mr Smith's suitcase = the suitcase of Mr Smith
6 the monkeys' bananas = the bananas of the monkeys
7 Mrs Jones' cat = the cat of Mrs Jones
8 the women's bags = the bags of the women
9 the people's choice = the choice of the people
10 the cows' barn = the barn of the cows
11 someone's hat = the hat of someone
12 anybody's guess = the guess of anybody

Step 2: If the spelling of the owner ends in 's', use an apostrophe after the 's' (s'). If not, use an apostrophe before the 's' ('s).

- Whether the owner is singular or plural isn't important. For example, notice above that in example 7, Mrs Jones is singular and yet the apostrophe comes after the 's' because 'Jones' ends in 's'.
- Also note that 'children' in example 4, 'women' in example 8 and 'people' in example 9 are plurals, but because they don't end in 's', they take the apostrophe before the 's'.

Exceptions: Words with Latin 'us' endings, such as 'fungus' and 'radius', use an apostrophe before the 's' in both the singular and plural. For example, in the singular, 'the spores of the fungus' becomes 'the fungus's spores', while in the plural, 'fungus' becomes 'fungi', so the possessive for 'the spores of the fungi' would be 'the fungi's spores'.

Have a GO! Ans p.109

1 Turn the following examples around and put the apostrophe in the correct place. For example: the craters of the moon = the moon's craters

a the shadow of the cloud ______________________

b the masks of the men ______________________

c the balls of the players ______________________

d the toys of the babies ______________________

e the dolls of the girl ______________________

f the cars of Robert ______________________

g the squeals of the mice ______________________

h the bellowing of the cows ______________________

i the house of Mr Evans ______________________

j the cottage of Mrs Robinson ______________________

k the pond of the hippopotamus ______________________

l the feathers of the geese______________________

m the wings of the ducks ______________________

2 Add apostrophes where they are needed in the following sentences.

a After Bobs party, we went to the cinema.

b I like the writers style in the book we just read.

c In the science class, we learnt about some famous scientists lives.

d What are the students opinions on this matter?

e Dickens books are harder to read than modern books.

f Shakespeares plays are even harder to understand.

g James brother, Peter, is the dux of his class.

h The pupils desks have all been painted.

i Kylies parents are overseas.

j In the school play, the womens parts were played by the boys.

k The surgeons gloves were torn, so he asked for new ones.

l One years work is not enough to pass this course.

m When Janes house was robbed, she felt scared to be alone.

n Bens liking for baggy trousers is peculiar.

o Somebodys coat was left here last night.

p Maxs swimming is a pleasure to watch.

q Yesterdays mail arrived at 3 o'clock.

r We should comb Montys fur every day.

22

Syllables and hyphens

Syllables

What are they?

Syllables are the **separate units of sound** that make up a word.

Examples of words with one syllable are:

bread, milk, cheese, fruit, yes, no, gun, egg, mouse, friend, book.

Examples of words with two or more syllables are:

mo-ther, dis-ap-pear, mis-un-der-stand.

Cutting words into syllables usually involves breaking the word between two consonants (e.g. yesterday = yes-ter-day, witness = wit-ness, window = win-dow). If two consonants aren't present next to each other, cut the word after the vowel (e.g. water = wa-ter, unit = u-nit, uniform = u-ni-form, giraffe = gi-raffe, female = fe-male).

The rules for syllabification are complex, however, and it is usually best to use your dictionary, if you are uncertain as to where to put the break.

Hyphens

What are they?

Hyphens are used:

- in many **compound words** that are used as adjectives (e.g. well-bred, never-to-be-forgotten, manly-looking, labour-saving, self-starter, hard-working)
- between **compound numbers** (e.g. thirty-two, forty-nine, eighty-one)
- between **fractions** (e.g. two-fifths, four-ninths, one-third, three-quarters)
- between **double nouns, adjectives and verbs** (e.g. actor-manager, well-nigh, dry-clean, cleaner-labourer, blue-green, stir-fry)
- to show the **interruption of a word** being carried over to the next line — the hyphen must be placed between syllables, not at random (e.g. fic-tion, not ficti-on; photo-graphy, not ph-otography).

Have a GO! Ans p.109

Put hyphens where you think they are needed in the following:

1 First we went on the merry go round and then we went on the see saw.

2 If you hurt yourself, an ice pack can reduce the swelling and bruising.

3 In the weekends, I love to play table tennis.

4 If you're in a rush, you can buy ready made sandwiches from the shop.

5 I put the boiled egg into the egg cup, and then I turned the egg timer off.

6 Maria has brown eyes, but Matt's are blue grey.

7 Three quarters of the children in the class have pets, which makes twenty two in all.

8 We went to the music hall to see a show and have dinner.

9 If you walk along the sea shore at low tide, you will see many beautiful sea shells.

10 The police had a search warrant to enter and search the house.

23

Composition

What are they?

To become a good writer, a student needs to think about the **purpose of the writing**, the **audience** to which it is being directed and the **type of language** required to make the writing effective. Think about the following types of compositions:

- For a set of **instructions**, a **procedure** or a **recipe**, the language needs to be clear and simple, and the layout should be in step-by-step, chronological order.
- For a **scientific report**, a special format must be followed to include an aim, method, results and conclusion. The language used must be technical and precise.
- For an **argumentative essay**, points for and against all sides of the argument must be examined, and a position should be taken and supported by evidence to persuade the reader. Formal language should be used throughout.
- For a **narrative, recount** or **story**, an introduction, development, a possible climax and a conclusion should be used. The language should be clear and concise, and the story should unfold in a logical sequence.

Learning how to compose good stories, essays and reports takes time and a lot of practice, but if the following basic rules are followed, your writing should be effective:

1 Always start your story, essay or report with an **introduction**. The introduction tells the reader what the story, essay or report will be about. It may set the scene or the time of the story or, in the case of an essay or report, describe the topic to be examined.

2 After the introduction, fill out **the body** of the story, essay or report. The body is the main part of the work. It can also be called the **development**. In a story, the action and characters are described, and the story unfolds in all its detail. In the case of an essay or report, the body describes, discusses, compares, argues or explains the topic clearly and in a logical order.

3 Towards the end of a story, there is usually a **climax**, which is the fastest and most exciting part of the story. It is often quite short but very dramatic. Essays and reports differ from stories as they usually do not have a climax. Instead, an essay may lead to a **decision** or **point of view**, and a report may show **results** of experiments or tables and diagrams to summarise and clarify information.

4 At the end of a story, a **conclusion** is used to complete it and round it off smoothly. In an essay or report, the conclusion briefly summarises the topic, gives a final opinion or recommendation, and may mention points for further study.

5 In an essay or report, it is common for a **bibliography** to be included after the conclusion, to show what books or other resources were used for gaining information. For each work listed in the bibliography you should give the title, author, publisher and year of printing.

Example

Look at this brief story of 'The Three Little Pigs', to see how it is split into introduction, body, climax and conclusion.

Introduction: Mother Pig has three young pigs who have grown up and need to find homes of their own. They leave home to seek their fortunes.

Body: The First Little Pig builds a house of straw, the Second Little Pig builds a house of sticks and the Third Little Pig builds a house of bricks. Then along comes the Big Bad Wolf. He blows down the First Little Pig's house of straw and eats him up. Next, he blows down the Second Little Pig's house of sticks and eats him up as well. Then he goes to blow down the Third Little Pig's house, but it is too strong. The Big Bad Wolf tells the Third Little Pig that he is going to get him by coming down the chimney!

Climax: The wolf starts to climb the chimney and while he is doing this, the Third Little Pig puts a pot of water on to boil in the fireplace. Finally the Big Bad Wolf comes hurtling down the chimney, only to splash into the boiling pot and be cooked.

Conclusion: The Third Little Pig eats Wolf Stew for dinner, and lives happily ever after.

1 Write a brief story of 'Little Red Riding Hood', breaking it up into its introduction, body, climax and conclusion, just as has been done above. Ask a parent or teacher to look at your work and correct it with you.

2 Write an **argumentative essay** examining all sides of the following statement:

The sooner the world uses nuclear electricity as its main source of energy the better. There will be no more greenhouse gases, no more oil spills, and breeder reactors will recycle the waste into further energy. Solar energy is too weak and unreliable to provide for our future needs.

GO!

3 Write a **report** on 'Jupiter and Its Great Red Spot', after doing the necessary research to gain as much information as you can on the topic. Remember to start with an **introduction**, move to the **body** of the report and finish with a **conclusion**. Make sure you set your work out in a logical order and include a bibliography at the end of your work.

4 Write a **book review** of your favourite book, keeping the rules of composition in mind. Start with details of title, author, publisher and, if known, date of first publication. Then discuss the **plot** (story), the **theme** (does the book have a deeper meaning beneath the story itself?), the **main characters** (the most important people in the story), and the **language** (modern or old-fashioned, simple or complex, formal or casual English). Give your **feelings and ideas** about the book, and conclude the review by giving your rating of it. Indicate to whom you would **recommend** the book, taking the age, sex and interests of the possible reader into account.

5 Write a **scientific report** after performing the following experiment at home to see how long it will take milk to turn thick and sour (like yoghurt). You are to test three separate, uncovered, 50 ml containers of milk under different conditions: one in the fridge, one at room temperature and one boiled (take care!) and left to cool in the open. Which one goes bad first? Which one takes the longest to go bad? Keep accurate notes of the experiment and, when it is finished, write your report, remembering to use the correct format of **aim, method, results** (possibly including photos or tables) and **conclusion**.

6 Write an **imaginative story** on 'The Fifth Dimension and How I Got There'. Remember to use an introduction, body, climax and conclusion, and make your story exciting and imaginative.

Writing technique

Avoid very long sentences

Young, inexperienced writers often string long sentences together with too many conjunctions. Generally, once a conjunction has been used in a sentence, finish off the second part of the sentence and begin a new sentence to continue.

Don't do this: Sandy and Steven came to Australia from China and settled in Sydney and went to college to learn to speak English and changed their names from Chinese names to their present English ones, so that people wouldn't have trouble remembering them. (This sentence is too long and has too many conjunctions).

This is better: Sandy and Steven came to Australia from China. They settled in Sydney and went to college to learn to speak English. Because their former Chinese names were difficult for people to remember, they changed them to their present English ones. (These sentences sound much more fluent).

Avoid repetition

Try not to repeat words, especially in openings to sentences. Choose different ways to begin sentences, making use of adjectival, adverbial and noun phrases. Avoid opening sentences all the time with 'then' or 'next', as your writing will become monotonous. If a word needs to be repeated in a sentence, choose a **synonym** (similar word) rather than repeat the same word. The sentence will sound much more elegant.

Don't do this: Ian and Daniel went to the Royal Easter Show and went on some scary rides. Then they went to buy some show bags, and then they went to see the animals, and then they went to see the big, giant pumpkins in the Vegetable Hall. Then they went to the wood-chopping and then they went to the Ring to see the car stunts. (These sentences sound boring with the constant repetition of 'and then they went to see'. This sort of writing is enough to put any reader to sleep!)

This is better: Ian and Daniel visited the Royal Easter Show. First they went on some scary rides and then they bought a few show bags. The animals were next on their list, followed by the big, giant pumpkins in the Vegetable Hall. The boys made sure they were in time for the wood-chopping, and their final stop was the Ring where the stunt cars were in action. (This group of sentences avoids the repetition of words and phrases by using synonyms. An effort is also made to open sentences in different ways, to keep the reader interested.)

Use pronouns carefully

When using a pronoun, make sure it is clear to which noun the pronoun refers. Generally, the noun will have been introduced in a previous sentence or earlier in the same sentence, before being referred to by a pronoun.

Don't do this: When I was four years old, I started having swimming lessons at our local pool. He was my teacher and a very good one too, because he had taught children how to swim for over twenty years. Mr Laidlaw had also been a life-saver. (The reader doesn't know who 'he' is until the third sentence is reached. This causes confusion and is difficult to read.)

Do this: When I was four years old, I started having swimming lessons at our local pool. Mr Laidlaw was my teacher and a very good one too, because he had taught children how to swim for over twenty years. He had also been a life-saver. (These sentences are easier to understand and the language flows more smoothly.)

Avoid splitting infinitives

Generally, you should not split infinitives (to run, to jump, to go, to be) by inserting other words between the 'to' and the verb.

Don't do this: We were told to *not* go home.

Do this: We were told *not* to go home.

Avoid separating closely linked parts of a sentence

Poor writers sometimes split one part of a sentence off from another closely related section, causing loss of clarity. Good writing is clear and simple, and shouldn't cause confusion to the reader. Look at the following examples to see how split constructions can cause awkward writing.

Awkward: After Mary had made her decision, she would, no matter what anybody did to stop her, not change her mind.

Improved: After Mary had made her decision, she would not change her mind, no matter what anybody did to stop her.

Awkward: Mrs Evans, with an almighty scream, climbed onto the chair to escape the mouse.

Improved: With an almighty scream, Mrs Evans climbed onto the chair to escape the mouse.

Awkward: Although Heather was a good pianist, she was never invited to play for the assembly, even though she practised daily.

Improved: Although Heather was a good pianist and practised daily, she was never invited to play for the assembly.

Don't dangle phrases

When a phrase is linked to a subject, make sure the phrase and its subject are close together, for clarity. If the phrase and its subject are separated by other words, the phrase is said to be 'dangling' and the meaning of the sentence is ambiguous, and often even silly!

Dangling: The watch was fixed by the jeweller with the damaged face.

Correct: The watch with the damaged face was fixed by the jeweller.

Dangling: Kim borrowed a chair from the neighbour with metal legs.

Correct: Kim borrowed a chair with metal legs from the neighbour.

Dangling: I saw a wombat running home from the shops this morning.

Correct: Running home from the shops this morning, I saw a wombat.

Dangling: Opening the door, the heat of the sauna struck me. (The heat didn't open the door. I did).

Correct: Opening the door, I was struck by the heat of the sauna.

Also correct: As I opened the door, the heat of the sauna struck me.

Dangling: On reading the newspaper, it was found to be full of bad news. (The newspaper didn't read itself. I read it).

Correct: On reading the newspaper, I found it to be full of bad news.

Also correct: When I read the newspaper, it was found to be full of bad news.

Use paragraphs to make your writing clearer

Your writing will be easier to follow if you use paragraphs:

- to separate the introduction, body, climax and conclusion;
- to separate changes of scene or time;
- to separate different topics or different aspects of a topic.

Choose a tense and stick to it

- Most stories and reports are written in the **past tense**, telling about what has already happened. Occasionally, a story is written in the present or future tense, but the past tense is the main tense for writing.
- Once you have chosen a tense for your writing, stay in that tense. Don't keep changing from one tense to the other, as it produces disjointed, uncomfortable writing.

Write in a logical sequence

Don't jump around in time, or order of events, during a story or report, unless there is a very good reason for doing so. Writing in a logical, step-by-step order will help the reader understand more clearly what you are trying to say.

Write in a formal style, unless there is a good reason not to

All stories and reports should be written in your **best, clearest English**, without the use of slang, abbreviations or poor grammar. Be very careful to check your work for good spelling, punctuation and paragraphing as well. The only times you might want to write informally are if you think your story will be made more realistic with less formal language, or if you are writing a letter to a friend.

Don't use grandiloquence or verbosity

Grandiloquence is the use of difficult or unfamiliar words for the purpose of trying to impress the reader. Verbosity (or wordiness) is the use of too many unnecessary words and is not good English. Using long, complicated sentences instead of simple, concise ones is bad practice. Some people think that by using a thesaurus to find a difficult word instead of a simple word, they will make their writing seem more sophisticated, but they are wrong. **Simple, concise, fluent English** is what you should be aiming for. This does not mean that you should use the same few words over and over again, however. Use as big a **variety of words** as you can to express yourself well and make your writing clear, but don't be a 'word show-off' just for the sake of it.

Study the notes on writing technique on pages 77–80, and then try to do as many of the following compositions as you can. Remember, the more you practise, the more your writing will improve. If you can, show your work to a parent or teacher, let them correct all your mistakes, including all spelling, punctuation, grammar and composition errors, and ask them to explain what you did wrong and how to improve your work. Make a list of your commonly made mistakes, and check this list before you write your next composition. By keeping your mistakes in mind, and trying to avoid repeating them, you will make real progress.

Imaginative stories (narratives)

1 A day in the life of a $2 coin
2 My journey in a time machine
3 The great Canberra earthquake of 2012
4 If I were the prime minister …
5 My life as a pet dog
6 The genie of the lamp and my three wishes

Descriptive paragraphs

1 The smell, as you pass a cake shop, of freshly cooked cakes or hot bread
2 The taste of your favourite food
3 The view as you gaze out from the summit of Mount Everest
4 The sound of a dripping tap, as you try to sleep at night
5 Your fear, as you realise that your parachute has failed!
6 The feeling of a raw egg being squished between your fingers

Research and factual accounts

1 The planet you find most interesting and why
2 A film review of the best film you've seen this year
3 Everyday life in Nepal
4 The life and times of Henry VII, King of England
5 A scientific report on the following experiment:
Add some milk to a saucer. Gently drop 2 or 3 drops of food dye onto the milk. Carefully add 1 drop of liquid washing-up detergent to the surface of the milk. Watch what happens for at least a minute. Repeat the procedure and then describe what you have observed. Think of a possible reason for the observations. Write clearly in scientific style.

Argumentative and discussion essays

1 Write a logical argument in support of the following topic:
'That too many video games and too much television are bad for the young mind'.
2 Analyse the following comment and give your opinion on it:
'Learning about history is pointless. Why would I want to know about a whole lot of dead people?'
3 Discuss the following idea: 'The Internet will soon make teachers redundant. We will be able to teach ourselves at home and will have more time with our friends and family.'

Stories with a particular beginning

Start stories with the following introductions, and use your imagination to develop and complete them.

1 The chest lay in a dark corner of the attic, covered in dust and cobwebs. For how long it had remained undisturbed, nobody knew, but I was about to find out what was hidden inside …
2 With eyes tightly shut, I held my breath and waited …
3 Leonardo da Vinci, greatest genius of mediaeval times, had been brought into the present and was going to spend a whole day with me. What would I show him of our modern world?

Stories with a particular ending

Write stories that end with these final sentences:

1 … Never, ever, again, will I make the same mistake!
2 … As the alien rocket took off, I knew that nobody would ever believe me.
3 … It's not until you face such a challenge that you realise how much bravery and strength lie within you.
4 … Queer, isn't it?

Writing letters

There are two main styles for writing letters:

- Letters to friends and family are written in a casual, relaxed style.
- Business letters and letters to newspapers are written in a formal style.

There are a few rules to learn about layout, when it comes to writing letters.

Letters to friends

When writing to friends or family, use **informal, simple language**, and write as though you were speaking to the person **in a conversation.** The layout of the letter should include:

- your address and the date in the top right-hand corner of the page;
- a blank line below the address;
- on the left of the page a greeting such as 'Dear Debbie/Mum/Uncle Tom' and the rest of the line left blank;
- a capital letter for the first word of the first paragraph;
- casual, relaxed language for the letter;
- at the end of the letter a friendly good-bye such as 'With love from', 'All the best' or 'Till next time';
- your name on the next line down.

12 Smith St
Sunbeam Cove
NSW 2983
29th February

Dear Paul

It was great to spend the holidays with you on your farm. If I'd stayed at home, I would never have had so much fun.

The night we went out on the boat at midnight and saw all the fluorescent lights in the water was fantastic. I never knew such a strange and beautiful thing could happen like that.

Justin arrived from France two days after we got home and you should have heard what he'd been eating. Frogs' legs and snails! He'll be able to have a big feast of them down at your pond, next time we come to visit you.

Mum's just finished the jumper she promised she'd make for you and she'll post it down to you soon.

Thanks again for a great time at your place.

Your mate

Sam

Whether you write a letter by hand or on the computer, the general layout is the same. The main difference between a hand-written and a computer-printed letter (or report) is in the **layout of paragraphs.** On a computer, if the letter is long, the clarity and appearance of the writing may be improved by leaving a blank line between each paragraph, rather than by indenting the first word.

With friendly letters, the writer can have fun choosing a different font or by inserting pictures to make the letter more personalised. With business letters, however, a conservative font and formal layout should be followed.

Business letters

Business letters should be written in **clear, formal English**, and you should make sure they are concise and laid out in a logical order. Don't use complicated language, just clear, simple vocabulary that states your meaning precisely. If you are writing a letter of complaint, be polite in your criticism, and if you can offer constructive suggestions, all the better. Be careful not to write something that you may regret later.

The layout of the letter is similar to the friendly letter, with a few extra details to note:

- Put your address and the date in the top right corner.
- Put the name (if known) and title of the person to whom you are writing (the addressee), on the left of the page, followed by their address.
- Leave a line blank below the address.
- Include a brief summary of the subject of the letter, starting with 'Re:', which means 'About'.
- Use a greeting such as 'Dear Dr Brown' or, if the person's name is not known, then 'Dear Sir/Madam'.
- Use formal, concise language for the letter.
- Use a good-bye in one of the following forms:
  - If you know the addressee's name, use 'Yours sincerely'.
  - If you only know the title but not the name of the addressee, use 'Yours faithfully' .
- Sign your name in your own handwriting, even if you have also printed your name out using the computer.

55 Possum Crescent
Fairydalc
NSW 2546
30th September

The Chief Astronomer
Sydney Observatory
1 Observatory Hill
Sydney NSW 2000

Re: Comet on possible collision course with earth.

Dear Sir/Madam

I am a very keen amateur astronomer, with eighteen years' experience in studying comets. I have been watching the skies over the past few nights and have been disturbed by some calculations I have made, concerning a new sighting.

I'm sure you must be aware of this new comet as well. I am writing to you to verify its motions, about which I am greatly concerned. By my calculations, it is on a direct path with Earth and is due to strike us on 17th October next year. Being an amateur, I assume I have made some ridiculous error, and that we have nothing to worry about. However, I have had a lot of experience over the years and have always been very accurate in my arithmetic.

Could you please let me know more details about this new sighting, and put my mind at ease about our impending doom.

Yours faithfully

Mrs Kathy Chadwick

24

Countries of the world

The following table shows the words we use to name some countries, capitals, languages and nationalities. Everyone should know these, as part of good general knowledge.

Country	Capital	Language	Person	The people
Australia	Canberra	English	Australian	The Australians
New Zealand	Wellington	English	New Zealander	The New Zealanders
Britain	London	English	Briton	The British
Scotland	Edinburgh	English	Scot	The Scots
England	London	English	Englishman/woman	The English
Wales	Cardiff	English	Welshman/woman	The Welsh
Ireland	Dublin	English	Irishman/woman	The Irish
Canada	Ottawa	English	Canadian	The Canadians
United States	Washington DC	English	American	The Americans
France	Paris	French	Frenchman/woman	The French
Germany	Berlin	German	German	The Germans
The Netherlands	Amsterdam	Dutch	Dutchman/woman	The Dutch
Switzerland	Bern	German	Swiss man/woman	The Swiss
Austria	Vienna	German	Austrian	The Austrians
Italy	Rome	Italian	Italian	The Italians
Spain	Madrid	Spanish	Spaniard	The Spanish
Portugal	Lisbon	Portuguese	Portuguese	The Portuguese
Greece	Athens	Greek	Greek	The Greeks
Russia	Moscow	Russian	Russian	The Russians
Poland	Warsaw	Polish	Pole	The Poles
Czech Republic	Prague	Czech	Czech	The Czechs
Hungary	Budapest	Hungarian	Hungarian	The Hungarians
Sweden	Stockholm	Swedish	Swede	The Swedes
Denmark	Copenhagen	Danish	Dane	The Danes
Norway	Oslo	Norwegian	Norwegian	The Norwegians
Finland	Helsinki	Finnish	Finn	The Finns

Country	Capital	Language	Person	The people
Iceland	Reykjavik	Icelandic	Icelander	The Icelandics
China	Peking	Mandarin	Chinese man/woman	The Chinese
Japan	Tokyo	Japanese	Japanese	The Japanese
Korea	Seoul	Korean	Korean	The Koreans
India	Delhi	Hindi	Indian	The Indians
Thailand	Bangkok	Thai	Thai	The Thais
Indonesia	Jakarta	Indonesian	Indonesian	The Indonesians
Malaysia	Kuala Lumpur	Malay	Malaysian	The Malaysians
Turkey	Ankara	Turkish	Turk	The Turks
Iraq	Baghdad	Arabic	Iraqi	The Iraqis
Iran	Tehran	Persian	Iranian	The Iranians
Egypt	Cairo	Arabic	Egyptian	The Egyptians
Israel	Jerusalem	Hebrew	Israeli	The Israelis
Brazil	Brasilia	Portuguese	Brazilian	The Brazilians
Argentina	Buenos Aires	Spanish	Argentine	The Argentines
Chile	Santiago	Spanish	Chilean	The Chileans

Once you have learnt the list above, you should be able to fill in the blanks below, without looking back:

Country	Capital	Language	Person	The people
Australia	Canberra	English	Australian	The Australians
New Zealand		English	New Zealander	The New Zealanders
Britain		English		The British
Scotland		English	Scot	The Scots
England	London	English		The English
Wales		English		The
Ireland		English	Irishman	The
Canada		English	Canadian	The Canadians
United States		English	American	The Americans
France		French		The French
Germany		German	German	The Germans
The Netherlands		Dutch		The Dutch
Switzerland	Bern		Swiss woman	The
Austria			Austrian	The Austrians
Italy		Italian	Italian	The Italians
Spain		Spanish		The

Country	Capital	Language	Person	The people
Portugal		Portuguese	Portuguese	The Portuguese
Greece		Greek	Greek	The
Russia		Russian	Russian	The Russians
Poland		Polish		The
Czech Republic		Czech	Czech	The Czechs
Hungary		Hungarian	Hungarian	The Hungarians
Sweden		Swedish		The
Denmark		Danish		The
Norway		Norwegian	Norwegian	The Norwegians
Finland			Finn	The
Iceland		Icelandic		The
China				The Chinese
Japan		Japanese	Japanese	The Japanese
Korea		Korean	Korean	The Koreans
India			Indian	The Indians
Thailand			Thai	The
Indonesia		Indonesian	Indonesian	The Indonesians
Malaysia			Malaysian	The Malaysians
Turkey			Turk	The
Iraq		Arabic	Iraqi	The
Iran		Persian	Iranian	The Iranians
Egypt		Arabic	Egyptian	The Egyptians
Israel	Jerusalem		Israeli	The
Brazil			Brazilian	The Brazilians
Argentina	Buenos Aires		Argentine	The
Chile	Santiago		Chilean	The Chileans

25

Phonics summary

Phonics summary

To be a good speller and reader, it is important to learn the spelling rules. Having a good knowledge of phonics (the sounds used in words) is essential. Do you know all these?

Letters	Examples	Sound
-ai-	rain, Spain, hail, snail, pain, afraid	Long A
-ay	day, play, stay, clay, Monday	
-a-e	cake, snake, shade, spade, female	
-ee	tree, see, bee, queen, deep, sleep, between	Long E
-ea-	mean, pea, team, cream, cheat, jeans	
-ie-	thief, belief, grief, chief	
-y	funny, sunny, happy, tasty, rainy, country	
-ey	donkey, journey, money, honey, valley	
-i-e	time, wipe, stripe, bike, like, mine, lie, tie	Long I
-ig	sigh, tight, right, thigh, tonight, sign, resign, design	
-y	try, shy, sly, cry, spy, why, fry, by, sky	
-ow	grow, show, window, pillow, throw	Long O
-o-e	phone, tone, home, choke, stole, toe	
-o	potato, tomato, mango, piano, go, yoyo	
-oa-	boat, float, goat, coat, cloak, moan, oats	
-u-e	tune, fortune, perfume, costume, refuse, cute, cure, mature	Long U
-ew	few, stew, pewter, dew, new, hew, nephew	
ph	phone, elephant, phantom	F
wh	what, when, where, why, whistle, whale, white	W
-ce, ci	dance, France, nice, space, cement, peace, police, city, excite	S
ps-	psalm, psychology, pseudonym	
-ge, gi	fridge, hedge, germ, college, knowledge, giraffe, giant, gin	J
-le	little, sample, dimple, battle	L
kn-	knee, know, knuckle	N
gn-	gnat, gnaw, gnash, gnome	
gh-	ghost, gherkin, ghastly, ghetto, ghoul	G

Letters	Examples	Sound
pt-	pterodactyl, ptarmigan, Ptolemy	T
-o-	colour, constable, wonderful, covenant, government, slovenly	U
-a-	wander, squander, what, swallow, squatter, watch, wattle	O
ch	chop, chum, bunch, church, change, reach, beach	Hard CH
-ture	picture, creature, future, feature, nature	
sh	ship, shop, shape, wish, fish, dish, shallow, she	Soft SH
-ci	special, racial, facial, spacious, delicious, gracious, malicious	
-ti	spatial, palatial, facetious, fiction, fraction, creation	
-ssi	mission, fission, passionfruit, recession, confession, session	
-si	television, derision, vision, incision	Hard ZSH
th	think, thanks, tooth, broth, throne, throw, maths	Soft TH
th	the, that, this, those, then, there	Hard TH
-oo	book, took, look, mistook, cook, foot, soot	Short OO
-oo	broom, room, tooth, boot, scooter, fool, tool, moon	Long OO
-ui	fruit, suit, juice	
-ew	chew, crew, threw, flew, jewellery, sewer	
-u-e	June, prune, flute, true, argue, glue, blue, cruel, fuel	
-oi-	join, coin, spoil, soil, oil, hoist, moist, point, ointment	OY
-oy	boy, toy, joy, annoy, oyster, alloy	
-ar	far, star, March, tart, smart, hard, art, bark	AR
-a-	fast, master, plaster, last, past, task, mask, craft, draft, after, father, lather, path, bath	
-or	for, corn, torn, or, glory, story, short, pork	OR
-ore	shore, galore, chore, ore, more	
-oor	door, floor, poor	
-aw	claw, raw, straw, awful, paw, saw, law, draw, crawl	
-augh	taught, distraught, naughty, daughter, slaughter, caught	
-ough	thought, bought, brought, nought	
-al	ball, tall, hall, mall, all, fall, talk, walk	
-ng	king, song, lung, long, bang	NG
-nk	pink, stink, link, tank, thank, plonk, rink, think	NK
-ou-	shout, lout, house, mouse, pound	OW
-ow	now, how, cow, clown, town, frown	
air	air, stairs, flair, fair, chair	AIR
-are	care, stare, mare, glare, dare	
-eer	steer, deer, veer, jeer, sneer, sheer, career	EAR
ear	ear, fear, hear, dear, tear	
-er	farmer, sister, swimmer, shopper, fatter, bigger, taller	ER
-ir	girl, swirl, squirt, shirt, flirt, dirt, fir, sir	
-ur-	burn, turn, hurt, urn, urgent, turtle, hurdle	

26

Good reading

Just as you learn good behaviour from the examples set by responsible adults, you also learn to write and speak in good English by reading the best examples that literature has to offer.

By reading the world's best books, you can:

- dramatically improve your knowledge of vocabulary
- increase your comprehension skills
- learn to express yourself in an intelligent, concise manner
- improve your powers of concentration
- enjoy exciting stories from different countries and various periods of history
- read about the lives and deeds of the world's greatest people
- stimulate your imagination
- improve your ability to think rationally and clearly
- escape into other worlds
- learn to feel for others
- explore the good and evil of human nature, so that you can learn right from wrong
- take part in discussions about the ideas and beliefs of the world's great thinkers.

These days, it is hard to get into the habit of reading, as there are so many distractions. Even when books are read, some of them are of a mediocre standard, using a limited vocabulary, colloquial English, slang, incorrect grammar, poor examples of behaviour, as well as dull or depressing plots and shallow characters. Books like this do not teach better standards of English or encourage a higher level of thinking.

Here is a list of some of the world's great books and stories. By choosing to read some of the works at a reading level at, or just beyond, your normal standard, you will slowly gain most, if not all, of the benefits listed above. **The more you read, the better your English will become.** Don't be scared of trying a book that seems a little difficult at first. It is only by pushing yourself beyond a comfortable limit that you will gain new vocabulary and improve your comprehension.

Good books for reading

Ruth Park, *Playing Beattie Bow*

Kenneth Grahame, *The Wind in the Willows*

George Eliot, *Silas Marner*

Mark Twain, *The Adventures of Huckleberry Finn*
Charles Dickens, *David Copperfield*
Charles Dickens, *A Tale of Two Cities*
Robert Louis Stevenson, *The Strange Case of Dr Jekyll and Mr Hyde*
Charlotte Brontë, *Jane Eyre*
Emily Brontë, *Wuthering Heights*
Robert Bolt, *A Man for All Seasons*
Albert Camus, *The Plague*
Jane Austen, *Pride and Prejudice*
Jane Austen, *Emma*
Daniel Defoe, *Robinson Crusoe*
Daniel Defoe, *Journal of the Plague Year*
Baroness Emmuska Orczy, *The Scarlet Pimpernel*
William Golding, *Lord of the Flies*
Aleksandr Solzhenitsyn, *One Day in the Life of Ivan Denisovich*
Jonathan Swift, *Gulliver's Travels*
George Orwell, *Animal Farm*
George Orwell, *Nineteen Eighty-Four*
Mary Shelley, *Frankenstein*
Martin Gardner, *The Ambidextrous Universe*
Richard Adams, *Watership Down*
Douglas Adams, *The Hitchhiker's Guide to the Galaxy*
Douglas Adams, *The Restaurant at the End of the Universe*
Franz Kafka, *Metamorphosis* (and other stories)
Edgar Allan Poe, *Tales of Mystery and Imagination*
John Wyndham, *The Seeds of Time*
H. G. Wells, *The Time Machine*
H. G. Wells, *The Invisible Man*
Jules Verne, *Journey to the Centre of the Earth*
Wilkie Collins, *The Moonstone*
Arthur Conan Doyle, *The Adventures of Sherlock Holmes*
William Bligh, *Mutiny on the Bounty*
Arthur Koestler, *The Sleepwalkers*
Anne Frank, *The Diary of a Young Girl*
Albert Marrin, *Hitler*
Albert Marrin, *Stalin: Russia's Man of Steel*
Helen Keller, *The Story of My Life*
Rachel Henning, *The Letters of Rachel Henning*

A good way to really appreciate a book, especially one written over forty years ago, is to find out the approximate year the book was written. Then, before starting the book, go to the library and find out from encyclopaedias and history books as much as you can about the history of the time, the scientific discoveries being made, the politics and philosophy of the era, the clothes being worn, the religion and customs of the country the book is based in, and information about the author of the book. By doing this, you will understand the book in greater depth and add to your general knowledge as well.

Answers for the Revision test are on pages 109–12.

1 Parts of speech

a The part of speech that acts as a naming word for people, places and things is the ______________.
Examples are ____

b The part of speech that acts as a doing, being or having word is the ____________
Examples are ____

c The part of speech that stands in place of a noun is the ________________.
Examples are ____

d The part of speech that describes nouns and pronouns is the ________________
Examples are ____

e The part of speech that describes verbs and sometimes adjectives and adverbs is the ________________.
Examples are ____

f The part of speech that acts as a joining word to make sentences longer is the __________________.
Examples are ____

g The part of speech that relates one noun with another and often refers to position is called the ______________________________.
Examples are ____

2 Composition

When writing stories, the composition should begin with an ____________________, which tells briefly what the story will be about. This should be followed by the __________________, in which the main part of the story is told. The most exciting part of the story is called the _______________, and it is usually quite short. The ending of the story is called the ____________________, in which the story is finished off and closed down. Every time one of these sections of the composition is begun, a new ______________________ should be used. Also, when the story moves from one topic or time to another, a new ______________________ should be started.

3 Nouns

Place the following nouns into the correct column in the table below.

dog, Mrs Brown, New Zealand, soup, desk, fleet, flock, the Queen, the River Nile, Wendy, dream, toe, Palaeozoic Era, sorrow, car, beauty, Blue-ringed Octopus.

Common	Proper	Collective	Abstract

4 Pronouns

Identify the types of pronouns underlined.

a Please pass <u>me</u> <u>that</u> and <u>I</u> will give <u>you</u> <u>this</u>.

__________, __________, __________, __________, __________,

b <u>Someone</u> stole my watch. ________________

c The crazy man stabbed <u>himself</u> with a knife. ________________

d This grammar text, <u>which</u> <u>you</u> are doing right now, is designed for students with good brains. __________, __________

e <u>Who</u> forgot their jumpers on such a cold day? ________________

f Einstein worked out the famous equation $e=mc^2$ <u>himself</u>. ________________

g <u>Each</u> of the children received money from the Tooth Fairy. ________________

h Ben and Adam tested <u>each other</u> before the exam. ________________

5 Gender and young

Complete the table below.

Masculine	Feminine	Young
	hen	
	duck	
dog		
	cat	
		foal
lion		
tiger		
	doe	
	goose	
		piglet
	swan	
king		
emperor		—
conductor		—
waiter		—
actor		—
aviator		—

6 Singular and plural

Give the plural for each of the following.

mouse ____________
house ____________
box ____________
sock ____________
peach ____________
child ____________
witch ____________
fungus ____________
nucleus ____________
radius ____________
mango ____________
tomato ____________
tornado ____________
piano ____________
photo ____________
zero ____________

index ____________
appendix ____________
vertex ____________
bacterium ____________
stadium ____________
medium ____________
phenomenon ____________
crisis ____________
oasis ____________
thief ____________
handkerchief ____________
loaf ____________
deer ____________
sheep ____________
moose ____________

7 Verbs

Give the different forms for each of these verbs.

Simple present	Simple past	Perfect	Past continuous	Future
jumps				
swims				
goes				
has				
is				
dreams				
brings				
buys				
lies				
lays				
sings				
makes				
bakes				
reads				
writes				

8 Voice

State whether the following sentences are in active or passive voice.

a Mary ran down the hill.

____

b Helen gave Donald a sausage.

____

c Spot was washed in the bath.

____

d Jack was invited to Angus' party.

____

e The leaking tap was fixed by the plumber.

____

f Sam has a bath at night.

____

9 Adjectives

Underline the adjectives in the sentences below and circle the nouns or pronouns they describe.

a Mean Mr Mustard is a miserly man.

b Little Miss Muffet was chased by a huge spider.

c The violent explosion was heard many miles away.

d The molten lava oozed down the side of the erupting volcano.

e The crooked man wore a crazy hat and owned a cranky cat.

Now cross out the **incorrect** adjective or adverb in the sentences below:

f Sally was real/very pleased to see Robert after such a long absence.

g I feel bad/badly when I think of my exam results.

h Mary spells bad/badly because she never studies her spelling book.

10 Prepositions

Underline the prepositions below.

The terrified children crept under the bed as they heard the maniac enter the room. The shuffling of feet came closer to them, so they crammed themselves further into the corner, when something peculiar happened. The surface of the wall seemed to be 'loose', and Tom noticed that he could put his hand straight through it. The maniac crouched down to look under the bed. Suddenly, in desperation, Tom grabbed Jill and dragged her through the wall. They had disappeared from the maniac's view. They were safe for now, but where were they? They had gone through the wall and come out, not in the next room, as Tom had hoped, but into a misty, dreamlike place that was totally alien to them. They had entered the 'Fourth Dimension'.

11 Adverbs

Underline the adverbs in the following sentences and state whether they are adverbs of time, manner or place.

a You go over and I'll go under. ______________________

b The children ran quickly home from the shops. ______________________

c Yesterday was my birthday. ______________________

d Jack arrived late for his ice-skating lesson. ______________________

e You will have to study hard to pass the exam. ______________________

f When you throw a rock up, it always comes back down. ______________________

12 Conjunctions

Underline the conjunctions in the following sentences.

a First we went on the Giant Slides, then we went on the Dodgems, next we went on the Turkey Trot and finally we went on the Rotating Disc.

b Although you weren't here when we arrived, we decided to wait for you.

c Wendy was hurt in a car crash, but she is getting better now.

d Since you are so disobedient to me, you will not get any more pocket money.

e Because the weather was bad, the show was postponed.

13 Sentences

State whether the following sentences are statements, questions, commands or exclamations, and place the correct punctuation at the end of each sentence, as needed.

a Go and make your bed before we go out ______________________

b What a fantastic skater you are ______________________

c How do you know which direction we should take ______________________

d Please make me a cup of tea, Adam ______________________

e Has Ginger come inside yet ______________________

f I've never heard such rubbish ______________________

g In the holidays, we will stay in a cabin ______________________

h How lovely the sunset looks ______________________

14 More verbs

Underline all the verbs, including auxiliary verbs, in the following sentences, and state what tense each sentence is in.

a We go to the shops on Fridays. ______________________

b Jack played at Ken's this weekend. ______________________

c Benn will go to college in two years' time. ______________________

d I have caught the chicken pox. ______________________

e We are going to the cinema on Tuesday. ______________________

f Adam had fallen over by the time I got there. ______________________

g Jack was riding his bike, when the storm started. ______________________

h Tina will be going on holidays to Switzerland. ______________________

i Sonia will have come home from school by now. ______________________

j Stephen and Gloria have eaten their dinner and done their homework. ______________________

____

15 Punctuation

Fill in any punctuation you think necessary in the following sentences.

a peter said to joran in a very soft voice wake up I think there is a burglar in the house

b for our picnic we packed bread chicken salad soft drink a blanket and swimmers

c i love playing boys games so please let me join in pleaded sarah

d the electrician who is working up inside the roof has to be careful not to electrocute himself

e no joanna you cant have everything you ask for

f although it was late the student was still revising for his test

g hard working people get more out of life

h blue green algae make oxygen for the atmosphere

16 Letter writing

Letter writing has a special layout. Write a short letter of thanks to a friend for a birthday present that you have received. Remember to include your address and the date and to give a correct start and finish to the letter.

17 Vocabulary

See how many words you know by filling in as many blanks as you can.

A home for a car: ____

A home for a plane: ____

A home for bees: ____

A home for fish: ____

A home for fruit trees: ____

A home for grapevines: ____

A home for a dog: ____

A home for criminals: ____

A home for soldiers: ____

A home for a king and queen: ____

A home for a horse: ____

A home for a ship: ____

A place to drink coffee: ____

A place to see a film: ____

A place to see a play: ____

A place to think about God: ____

A place to bury the dead: ____

A place to store wine: ____

A place where nuns live: ______

A place to see paintings: ______

A place to see historical relics: ______

A place where goods are made: ______

A place where bread is baked: ______

A place where fruit and vegetables are sold: ______

A place where you can ice-skate: ______

A place where you can play golf: ______

A place where you can do tenpin bowling ______

As black as ______

As brave as a ______

As thin as a ______

As quiet as a ______

As cunning as a ______

As white as ______

As sick as a ______

As blind as a ______

As busy as a ______

As gentle as a ______

A writer of books ______

A healer of the sick ______

A tooth doctor ______

An animal doctor ______

A mender of pipes ______

A fixer of electrical things ______

18 Mood

At the end of each sentence, state its mood.

a Go and wash the dishes now, please Matt. ______

b It is essential that you tell your parents what happened. ______

c The countryside looked beautiful, covered in a dusting of snow.

______

d If I were you, I'd give it back. ______

e How long is a piece of string? ______

19 Transitives and intransitives

Underline the verbs in the sentences below and state whether they are transitive or intransitive.

a Mary had a little lamb. ______

b Sarah cried and cried after her bad dream. ______

c Yoshi flew his kite high in the sky. ______

d I have a sore throat. ______

e I stayed awake until sunrise. ______

20 Subjects and predicates

Circle the subject and underline the predicate in the sentences below.

a The Man in the Moon came tumbling down from the sky.

b Do you like my new shoes?

c The submarine dived beneath the deep, blue sea.

d Eliza, Dick and Charles have gone to play tennis this afternoon.

e I'm too scared to rock-climb because I fear the rope might break.

21 Collective nouns

See if you can fill in the correct people, animals or objects that go with the following collective nouns.

A school of ______	A nest of ______
A congregation of ______	A brood of ______
A crowd of ______	A hive of ______
A flock of ______	A murder of ______
A fleet of ______	A spool of ______
A herd of ______	A pack of ______
A pod of ______	A bouquet of ______
An audience of ______	A cluster of ______
A band of ______	A galaxy of ______
A gang of ______	A collection of ______
A batch of ______	A ream of ______
A pride of ______	An aviary of ______
A litter of ______	A gaggle of ______
A battery of ______	An aquarium of ______

22 Story writing

Remembering your rules of good composition, choose one of the topics below and write the best story you can. It should be at least one page long.

a The time: AD 3567; the place: New York City

b The avalanche and how I survived it

c My million dollar fortune and how I would spend it

d The day the Sun died

e My dream house/car/holiday

f My future career

g The story of how the snake lost his legs

23 Parsing

Parse the following sentence, stating as much as you can about each word.

The incredibly enormous giant squashed the house with his foot.

24 Analysis

Analyse the following sentence by examining its different parts.

The Goblin told the Hobbit that his feet were too hairy.

Answers

1 Nouns

Page 2

Common	Proper	Collective	Abstract
star	Mrs Lee	group	beauty
saucer	Britain	fleet	horror
egg	the King of Spain	crowd	sport
boys	Monty	class	misery
sardines	Bondi	mob	heat
king	Perth	gang	democracy
dog	Wizard of Oz		wealth
fish	Kelloggs		comedy
apple			
desk			

Page 4

dog	dogs	crisis	crises
cat	cats	hippopotamus	hippopotami
peach	peaches	deer	deer
fox	foxes	sheep	sheep
puppy	puppies	ox	oxen
journey	journeys	piano	pianos
dwarf	dwarves	zero	zeros
wife	wives	photo	photos
mango	mangoes	house	houses
tomato	tomatoes	foot	feet
potato	potatoes	tooth	teeth
vertex	vertices	child	children
bacterium	bacteria	mouse	mice

1 The boys are riding their bikes up very steep hills.
2 The woman goes to the oasis with her ox and camel to fetch water.
3 The deer and sheep must be protected from the wolf in the woods.
4 We have boxes with peaches, mangoes, photos and sharks' teeth in them.
5 These books have appendices at the back.
6 Rhombi are like pushed-over squares.

Page 5

king	queen	uncle	aunt
prince	princess	man	woman
duke	duchess	husband	wife
knight	dame	actor	actress
lord	lady	waiter	waitress
emperor	empress	master	mistress
wizard	witch	aviator	aviatrix
hero	heroine	conductor	conductress
manager	manageress	god	goddess

Page 7

sheep	lamb	swan	cygnet
dog	pup	hen	chicken
duck	duckling	pig	piglet
goose	gosling	cow	calf
cat	kitten	whale	whale calf
deer	fawn	human	baby/child
horse	foal	plant	seedling
bird	nestling/fledgling	tree	sapling
goat	kid	flower	bud

2 Pronouns

Page 8

1 Jenny is a schoolgirl. She is six years old and she goes to Chatswood Public School, where she is in Year 1. She has a big brother called Mark. He is twelve and he loves cricket. His favourite food is noodles and he also loves going to the cinema.

2 **a** his*, it, him **b** you, you, he, you **c** he **d** this*, mine, that, yours, those, theirs **e** we, them, our* **f** nobody, me, it, your* **g** who

(*his head , this book, our lesson and your birthday look like pronouns but are, more correctly, adjectives. See p. 10.)

Page 10

1 demonstrative, demonstrative 2 emphatic 3 reflexive 4 personal 5 distributive 6 relative 7 interrogative 8 distributive, reciprocal 9 relative 10 indefinite 11 demonstrative, possessive 12 interrogative 13 personal, personal, personal 14 personal, reflexive

3 Adjectives

Page 11

1 This exercise has various answers, depending on student's own choices.

2 It was a wild and windy night and, as the wispy clouds sailed across the rising, yellow moon, I saw an ugly witch riding a bristly broomstick, her tall, pointed hat on her head, and a black cat with shining eyes resting on her shoulder. I could hear the witch's evil cackle as she flew off into the cold, midnight air.

Page 12

1 heavy (rain), descriptive 2 former (teacher), limiting; strict (teacher), descriptive; present (one) limiting; lenient (one), descriptive 3 first (child), limiting 4 small (ants), descriptive; powerful (ants), descriptive 5 eight (girls), limiting 6 most (clarity), limiting 7 hot (mud), descriptive 8 your (writing), possessive; untidy (writing); descriptive 9 every (boy), distributive 10 these (boxes), demonstrative 11 which (puppy), interrogative; cutest (puppy), descriptive

4 Verbs

Page 13 1 skis (doing), has (having) 2 is (being) 3 is (being) 4 does (doing) 5 has (having) 6 is (being) 7 should be (being) 8 skipped (doing), hopped (doing), jumped (doing) 9 sleep (doing) 10 study (doing), will pass (doing)

Page 14 1 present simple 2 past simple 3 past continuous 4 future simple 5 future continuous 6 present continuous 7 past simple 8 future simple 9 past continuous 10 future continuous

Page 15

Present	Past	Perfect	Future
have	had	have had	will have
am/are	was/were	have been	will be
go	went	have gone	will go
do	did	have done	will do
make	made	have made	will make
take	took	have taken	will take
shake	shook	have shaken	will shake
stand	stood	have stood	will stand
weep	wept	have wept	will weep
sleep	slept	have slept	will sleep
creep	crept	have crept	will creep
leap	leapt	have leapt	will leap
dream	dreamt	have dreamt	will dream
swim	swam	have swum	will swim
sing	sang	have sung	will sing
sink	sank	have sunk	will sink
stink	stank	have stunk	will stink
drink	drank	have drunk	will drink
think	thought	have thought	will think
buy	bought	have bought	will buy
bring	brought	have brought	will bring
write	wrote	have written	will write
say	said	have said	will say
lie	lay	have lain	will lie
lay	laid	have laid	will lay
draw	drew	have drawn	will draw
know	knew	have known	will know
blow	blew	have blown	will blow
throw	threw	have thrown	will throw
show	showed	have shown	will show
run	ran	have run	will run
speak	spoke	have spoken	will speak
strike	struck	have struck	will strike
eat	ate	have eaten	will eat
see	saw	have seen	will see
put	put	have put	will put
shut	shut	have shut	will shut
sew	sewed	have sewn	will sew
mean	meant	have meant	will mean
hide	hid	have hidden	will hide
drive	drove	have driven	will drive
ride	rode	have ridden	will ride
slide	slid	have slid	will slide
sit	sat	have sat	will sit

Page 17 1 been, happened 2 went 3 driven 4 lay 5 brought, bought 6 laid, lain 7 hid, waited 8 made 9 says, said 10 eat, ate, eaten 11 had, slept

Page 18 ***Simple past:*** 1 went 2 played 3 wrote 4 drove 5 laid 6 lay, had 7 was 8 could come 9 concentrated, ate 10 blew

Perfect: 1 have always gone 2 has played 3 have written 4 have driven 5 have laid 6 has lain, has had 7 has not been 8 have been able to come 9 have concentrated, have eaten 10 has blown

5 Adverbs

Page 20

1 **a** tomorrow (when) **b** faster (how) **c** violently (how) **d** too (how much), slowly (how), very (how much) **e** up (where), sweetly (how) **f** behind (where) **g** quietly (how) **h** quickly (how) **i** rudely (how) **j** quite (how much) **k** carefully (how)

2 **a** adv: cheerfully, skipped (manner) **b** adv: today, feel (time) **c** adv: slowly, worked (manner) **d** adv: today, are going (time), adv: nowhere, are going (place) **e** adv: almost, empty (quantity) **f** adv: spookily, howled (manner) **g** adv: incredibly, beautiful (quantity) **h** adv: never, eat (time) **i** adv: away, ran (place)

6 Comparatives and superlatives

Page 22

Positive	Comparative	Superlative
big	bigger	biggest
small	smaller	smallest
funny	funnier	funniest
beautiful	more beautiful	most beautiful
complicated	more complicated	most complicated
good	better	best
bad	worse	worst
much	more	most
little	less	least

Page 23 Correct words: 1 cold 2 coldly 3 awkward 4 awkwardly

7 Conjunctions

Page 24 1 but 2 and 3 because 4 whenever 5 although 6 since 7 than 8 although 9 whenever 10 and 11 because 12 and 13 but 14 so

Page 25 1 didn't come (because) wasn't invited 2 (whenever) go, rains 3 worked (and) came 4 (although) wrote, reply 5 raced (but) got 6 should have been told (that) would cost 7 must go (*understood*) (and) must go 8 can come (but) cannot (*understood*) 9 went (though) was setting 10 (if) can find, can keep 11 am coming (whether) like (or) do not like (*understood*) 12 (unless) get, will miss 13 (while) were, was delivered

8 Interjections

Page 26

1 I've told you a million times not to do that! (exclamation)
2 I get terrible hay fever in Spring. (statement)
3 That was the best film I've ever seen! (exclamation)
4 Fantastic! Your reading is really improving! (interjection, followed by exclamation)
5 Oh no! I forgot to bring the present! (interjection, followed by exclamation)
6 Have you done your Christmas shopping yet? (question)
7 Brilliant! I didn't know you could do that! (interjection, followed by exclamation)
8 My favourite animals at the zoo are the wombats and the apes. (statement)

9 Prepositions

Page 28 1 over 2 to 3 on 4 among 5 to 6 in 7 at 8 under 9 into 10 over 11 in 12 on 13 behind 14 with

10 Articles

Page 31 1 a, the 2 an 3 the, the 4 the, the, the, the, the, the 5 an *or* the (depends on context) 6 a, an 7 an, a, a

Page 32 1 — , — 2 a *or* the (depends on context) 3 a 4 — , — 5 — , — 6 — 7 the 8 a *or* the (depends on context) 9 — , — 10 a, a

11 Subjects, predicates and objects

Page 34

1. (Jack and Jill) ran up the hill.
2. (Steven and Sandy) live in Killara.
3. (Paola) watches television in the afternoons.
4. Because of the bad storm, (we) decided to stay home.
5. (The old tramp) used to sleep under this bridge.
6. (Tanya and Nick) go to the city every week.
7. (Tomcats) often fight at night.
8. How did (young Helen) break her arm?
9. Please bring me a can of oil. (you *understood*)
10. Suddenly, (the speeding driver) lost control and went over the cliff.

Page 35 1 (told) him; (to sell) cow 2 (sold) cow; (for) beans; (of) money 3 (sent) son; (to) bed; (in) disgrace 4 (threw) beans; (of) window 5 (in) morning; (up) beanstalk 6 (at) top; (of) beanstalk; (discovered) castle; (in) clouds 7 (owned) hen

12 More about verbs

Page 37 1 present simple 2 past simple 3 present perfect 4 past continuous 5 present simple 6 future simple 7 past perfect 8 future perfect 9 future continuous 10 present simple 11 present simple 12 past simple 13 future simple 14 past simple 15 present perfect continuous

Page 39 1 (told), to go *inf.* 2 clapping *pres,* (rose) 3 chained *past,* (could move) 4 (was playing) 5 (had ridden), telling *pres.*

Page 40 1 transitive (a bridge) 2 transitive (hot baths) 3 intransitive 4 intransitive 5 transitive (the sad news) 6 intransitive 7 transitive (the three-legged race) 8 intransitive 9 transitive (cars); transitive (love cars *understood)* 10 intransitive

13 Gerunds

Page 42 1 cheating 2 shouting 3 knowing 4 reading 5 writing ('reading' is a present participle) 6 (going), doing 7 (living), buying 8 speaking, (fearing) 9 Hiking, (hiking)

14 Phrases

Page 43 1 under the house (prep) 2 over the moon (prep) 3 cackling with laughter (pres. part), on her broomstick (prep) 4 to be late (infin), not to come at all (infin) 5 written in red ink (past part), for all to see (prep) 6 hidden somewhere (past part), among the crowd (prep), ticking away (pres. part) 7 under a tree (prep), on his head (prep) 8 writing neatly (ger), in your assignment (prep) 9 riding on the Rotor (ger), at Luna Park (prep)

Page 44 1 in the cage (adj) 2 in great terror (adv of manner), from the fire-breathing dragon (adv of place) 3 walking through the park at night (noun) 4 among the reeds (adv of place) 5 tired out after the long trip (adj) 6 building the dam (noun), plenty of water for the farmers' crops (noun) 7 to sleepwalk (noun) 8 to pull the sword from the stone (noun) 9 outside the village (adv of place), with a long, grey beard (adj) 10 used by the criminal (adj), in the cellar (adv of place), covered with blood (adj)

15 Person

Page 46 1 second sing. or plur. 2 third sing. 3 third sing. 4 third plur. 5 second plur. 6 first plur. 7 third sing. 8 third plur. 9 third sing. 10 third plur. 11 first sing. 12 first plur. 13 second plur.

16 Case

Page 48

1 subjective, objective, possessive, objective, possessive
2 subjective, objective, objective, possessive
3 objective, subjective, subjective (after the verb 'to be')
4 subjective, objective, subjective, subjective, subjective (after the verb 'to be')
5 subjective, subjective (after the verb 'to be'), objective, subjective, objective, subjective, possessive, objective

17 Converting to another part of speech

Page 49

Noun	Verb	Adjective	Adverb
enlargement/ largeness	enlarge	large	largely
danger	endanger	dangerous	dangerously
energy	energise	energetic	energetically
enjoyment	enjoy	enjoyable	enjoyably
talk	talk	talkative	talkatively
beauty	beautify	beautiful	beautifully
emptiness	empty	empty	—
embarrassment	embarrass	embarrassing/ed	embarrassingly
speed	speed	speedy	speedily
bravery	—	brave	bravely
quietness	quieten	quiet	quietly
peace	pacify	peaceful	peacefully
hatred	hate	hateful, hated	hatefully
fantasy	fantasise	fantastic	fantastically
horror	horrify	horrible	horribly
study, student	study	studious	studiously
glory	glorify	glorious	gloriously
life	live	lively	livelily
knowledge	know	knowledgeable	knowledgeably

18 Voice and mood

Page 52 1 active 2 passive 3 passive 4 active 5 passive 6 active

Page 53 1 indicative 2 interrogative 3 subjunctive 4 subjunctive 5 imperative 6 indicative 7 subjunctive 8 indicative 9 interrogative 10 subjunctive 11 subjunctive 12 imperative 13 subjunctive 14 subjunctive 15 subjunctive

19 Clauses

Page 55

1 I saw you (when you hid behind that tree).
2 That is the girl (who came top of the class).
3 We all know (that it is your birthday tomorrow).
4 Andy and Rachel always have dinner (after they have had a bath).
5 We were very sad (when those poor men died in the submarine).
6 William asked for pavlova, (because it is his favourite dessert).
7 Tadpoles live in the water and frogs live on the land.
8 This is my pet rat, (which sleeps in my slipper).
9 (While watching the long game of cricket), I fell asleep.
10 This is the house (where I was born).
11 You take the high road and I'll take the low road.
12 Be thankful (that you are fit and healthy).

Page 56 1 noun 2 adjectival 3 adverbial 4 noun 5 noun 6 adjectival 7 adverbial 8 adverbial 9 adverbial

20 Sentences

Page 58

1 We have a dog and two guinea pigs.
We: pronoun, personal, first person, plural, subjective case, subject of 'have'
have: verb, present simple tense, third person, plural, finite (subject = 'we'), transitive (object = 'dog', 'guinea pigs'), irregular conjugation, indicative mood, active voice
a: indefinite article, qualifying 'dog'
dog: noun, common, singular, common gender, objective case, object of 'have'
and: conjunction, joining 'We have a dog' with 'We have two guinea pigs'
two: adjective, limiting, qualifying 'guinea pigs'
guinea pigs: noun, common, plural, common gender, objective case, object of 'have'

2 Action films are spectacular to watch.
Action: adjective, descriptive, qualifying 'films'
films: noun, common, plural, neuter, subjective case, subject of 'are'
are: verb, present simple tense, third person, plural, finite (subject = 'films'), intransitive, irregular conjugation, indicative mood, active voice
spectacular: adjective, descriptive, qualifying 'films'
to watch: verb, infinitive, non-finite, intransitive

Page 59

1 We went to the Sushi Train for lunch, because we had heard how good it was.
Principal clause: We went to the Sushi Train for lunch
Subordinate clause 1: because we had heard (adverbial clause of reason, modifying 'went' in the principal clause)
Subordinate clause 2: how good it was (noun clause, object of 'had heard' in the adverbial clause)

2 In summer, Oki went to the Outback and Kathi visited Tasmania.
Principal clause 1: Oki went to the Outback
Principal clause 2: Kathi visited Tasmania
Conjunction: 'and', joining the two principal clauses
Adverbial phrase of time: In summer (modifying the verbs 'went' and 'visited')

Page 60 1 tick 2 cross 3 tick 4 cross 5 cross 6 tick 7 cross 8 cross 9 tick

Page 61 1 question 2 statement 3 command 4 exclamation 5 command 6 question 7 exclamation 8 exclamation 9 statement 10 command

21 Punctuation

Page 62

1 We went to the zoo on Saturday. (statement)
2 Have you been to the zoo recently? (question)
3 What a disgusting mess! (exclamation)
4 Peel the potatoes while I bath the baby. (command)
5 How old will you be this year? (question)
6 Do you own a Ford or a Holden? (question)
7 Please make your bed before breakfast. (command)
8 Have you made your bed yet? (question)
9 What a helpful girl you are! (exclamation)
10 Good children help their parents around the home. (statement)
11 What's your favourite song? (question)
12 Play the piano for us. (command)
13 Do you know how to play the violin? (question)
14 Most Korean children learn to play an instrument. (statement)
15 Well done, you clever girl! (exclamation)

Page 64 When I was a teenager, the men landed on the moon for the first time and it was so exciting. I was at school and we watched the men get out of their rocket. We were scared that the moon dust might be very soft and that the men might sink right under the surface. Luckily, that didn't happen. The men walked around collecting moon rocks and putting them in a bag, so that they could be studied back on Earth. Because gravity is less on the moon than on Earth, the men could jump very high, even with their heavy spacesuits on. Would you like to go to the moon one day? I would.

Page 66

1 We bought apples, pears, bananas and oranges for the fruit salad.
2 The dinosaur was a long-toothed, sharp-clawed, quick-footed, bloodthirsty, vicious monster.
3 Although we arrived early, the restaurant was full.
4 Diana, clean the duck's cage before you come inside.
5 Yes, you can put the Christmas tree up tomorrow.
6 My two sons, who like to stay up late, are always tired in the morning.
7 The magician did some magic tricks with a rabbit and a pack of cards, and then the acrobats went on the flying trapeze.
8 Believe it or not, I saw a pig fly past the window.
9 If you eat your vegetables, you may have dessert.
10 Lizards, snakes, tortoises and turtles are all reptiles.
11 Sean, you must tell the truth.
12 The boys, even the tall ones, were short compared with the basketball players.
13 I said no, but they came anyway.
14 If life is here on Earth, couldn't it be on other planets as well?
15 I think Rugby League players are great, big, stupid oafs!

16 To be honest with you, I really don't know.
17 The teacher said, 'Do your homework by Friday'.
18 'Get out of my room at once,' shouted Julia angrily.
19 Creeping quietly down the hall, the girl saw Father Christmas unloading presents.
20 Late at night, we sometimes look at the stars through our telescope.

Page 67

'What was Armstrong's pulse rate, when he set foot on the moon?' I asked.

'Oh! Surprisingly it was much lower than when he was landing in his rocket,' answered the NASA expert. 'The problem was that he was low on fuel, so low in fact, that if he hadn't landed when he did, he would have crashed.'

'Good grief!' I replied. 'They never told us that!'

'Well, he had only five seconds of fuel left, and his pulse rate was racing, as you can well imagine,' explained the man from NASA.

Page 69

1 Edward said, 'I tried my hardest to explain to her what had happened, but she yelled, 'Get out of my way. I never want to see you again!' so I went home feeling very depressed.'
2 'Which way do we go now?' screamed Michael.
'How should I know?' I yelled back. 'I've never been here before,' I reminded him.
'Yes you have!' screeched Michael, in a panicky voice.
3 Did you really believe the gypsy when she said, 'I can tell your future'?
4 I couldn't believe my luck when the man rang me and said, 'You've won the lottery'!

Page 71

1 **a** the cloud's shadow **b** the men's masks **c** the players' balls **d** the babies' toys **e** the girl's dolls **f** Robert's cars **g** the mice's squeaks **h** the cows' bellowing **i** Mr Evans' house **j** Mrs Robinson's cottage **k** the hippopotamus's pond **l** the geese's feathers **m** the ducks' wings
2 **a** Bob's party **b** writer's style **c** scientists' lives **d** students' opinions **e** Dickens' books **f** Shakespeare's plays **g** James' brother **h** pupils' desks **i** Kylie's parents **j** women's parts **k** surgeon's gloves **l** year's work **m** Jane's house **n** Ben's liking **o** somebody's coat **p** Max's swimming **q** yesterday's mail **r** Monty's fur

22 Syllables and hyphens

Page 74

1 merry-go-round, see-saw 2 ice-pack 3 table-tennis 4 ready-made 5 egg-cup, egg-timer 6 blue-grey 7 Three-quarters, twenty-two 8 music-hall 9 sea-shore, sea-shells 10 search-warrant

24 Countries of the world

Page 85

Check your answers from the table on pages 84–5.

27 Revision test

Page 91

1 a noun, e.g. Mark, egg, Australia, Easter, pencil, flock, beauty, dream
b verb, e.g. run, jump, skip, hop, do, be, have
c pronoun, e.g. I, you, he, they, we, us, them, mine, whose, nobody, ours
d adjective, e.g. pretty, long, five, yellow, many, funny
e adverb, e.g. yesterday, happily, away, soon, hungrily
f conjunction, e.g. and, but, because, since, although, or, whenever
g preposition, e.g. under, beneath, over, at, in, with, of, to, among

2 introduction, body (development), climax, conclusion, paragraph, paragraph

3

Common	Proper	Collective	Abstract
dog	Mrs Brown	fleet	dream
soup	New Zealand	flock	sorrow
desk	the Queen		beauty
toe	the River Nile		
car	Wendy		
	Palaeozoic Era		
	Blue-ringed Octopus		

4 **a** personal, demonstrative, personal, personal, demonstrative **b** indefinite **c** reflexive **d** relative, personal **e** interrogative **f** emphatic **g** distributive **h** reciprocal

5

Masculine	Feminine	Young
rooster/cockerel	hen	chicken
drake	duck	duckling
dog	bitch	pup
tom-cat	cat	kitten
stallion	mare	foal
lion	lioness	cub
tiger	tigress	cub
stag	doe	fawn
gander	goose	gosling
boar	sow	piglet
swan	swan	cygnet
king	queen	prince/princess
emperor	empress	—
conductor	conductress	—
waiter	waitress	—
actor	actress	—
aviator	aviatrix	—

6 mice, houses, boxes, socks, peaches, children, witches, fungi, nuclei, radii, mangoes, tomatoes, tornadoes, pianos, photos, zeros, indices, appendices, vertices, bacteria, stadia, media, phenomena, crises, oases, thieves, handkerchiefs, loaves, deer, sheep, moose

7

Present simple	Past simple	Perfect	Past continuous	Future
jumps	jumped	has jumped	was jumping	will jump
swims	swam	has swum	was swimming	will swim
goes	went	has gone	was going	will go
has	had	has had	was having	will have
is	was	has been	was being	will be
dreams	dreamt	has dreamt	was dreaming	will dream
brings	brought	has brought	was bringing	will bring
buys	bought	has bought	was buying	will buy
lies	lay	has lain	was lying	will lie
lays	laid	has laid	was laying	will lay
sings	sang	has sung	was singing	will sing
makes	made	has made	was making	will make
bakes	baked	has baked	was baking	will bake
reads	read	has read	was reading	will read
writes	wrote	has written	was writing	will write

8 **a** active **b** active **c** passive **d** passive **e** passive **f** active

9 **a** mean, miserly (Mr Mustard) **b** little (Miss Muffet), huge (spider) **c** violent (explosion), many (miles) **d** molten (lava), erupting (volcano) **e** crooked (man), crazy (hat), cranky (cat). The following are **incorrect**: **f** real **g** badly **h** bad

10 under, of, to, into, of, through, under, in, through, from, through, in, into, to

11 **a** over (place), under (place) **b** quickly (manner) **c** yesterday (time) **d** late (time) **e** hard (manner) **f** up (place), always (time), back (place), down (place)

12 **a** and **b** although **c** but **d** since **e** because

13 **a** command (full stop) **b** exclamation (exclamation mark) **c** question (question mark) **d** command (full stop) **e** question (question mark) **f** exclamation (exclamation mark) **g** statement (full stop) **h** exclamation (exclamation mark)

14 **a** go (present simple) **b** played (past simple) **c** will go (future simple) **d** have caught (present perfect) **e** are going (present continuous) **f** had fallen (past perfect), got (past simple) **g** was riding (past continuous), started (past simple) **h** will be going (future continuous) **i** will have come (future perfect) **j** have eaten (present perfect), have (*understood)* done (present perfect)

15 a Peter said to Joran, in a very soft voice, 'Wake up! I think there is a burglar in the house.'
b For our picnic, we packed bread, chicken, salad, soft drink, a blanket and swimmers.
c 'I love playing boys' games, so please let me join in,' pleaded Sarah.
d The electrician, who is working up inside the roof, has to be careful not to electrocute himself.
e No, Joanna. You can't have everything you ask for.
f Although it was late, the student was still revising for his test.
g Hard-working people get more out of life.
h Blue-green algae make oxygen for the atmosphere.

16 Ask a parent or teacher to look at your work and correct it with you.

17 garage, hangar, hive, aquarium, orchard, vineyard, kennel, gaol (jail), barracks, palace, stable, dock (wharf), café, cinema, theatre, church (*or* chapel, cathedral, synagogue, temple, mosque), cemetery (graveyard), cellar, convent (nunnery), art gallery, museum, factory, bakery, greengrocer, ice-rink, golf course (golf links), bowling alley, pitch, lion, rake, mouse, fox, snow, dog, bat, bee, lamb, author, doctor, dentist, vet (veterinarian), plumber, electrician

18 **a** imperative **b** subjunctive **c** indicative **d** subjunctive **e** interrogative

19 **a** had (transitive) **b** cried (intransitive) **c** flew (transitive) **d** have (transitive) **e** stayed (intransitive)

20 a (The Man in the Moon) <u>came tumbling down from the sky.</u>
b <u>Do</u> (you) <u>like my new shoes?</u>
c (The submarine) <u>dived beneath the deep, blue sea.</u>
d (Eliza, Dick and Charles) <u>have gone to play tennis this afternoon.</u>
e (I)<u>'m too scared to rock climb because I fear the rope might break.</u>

21 a school of fish
a congregation of worshippers
a crowd of people
a flock of sheep/birds
a fleet of ships
a herd cattle
a pod of whales
an audience of listeners
a band of musicians
a gang of thieves/hoodlums
a batch of scones
a pride of lions
a litter of puppies
a battery of weapons
a nest of birds
a brood of chickens
a hive of bees
a murder of ravens
a spool of thread
a pack of wolves/cards
a bouquet of flowers
a cluster of diamonds
a galaxy of stars
a collection of stamps
a ream of paper
an aviary of birds
a gaggle of geese
an aquarium of fish

22 Ask a parent or teacher to look at your work and correct it with you.

23 The incredibly enormous giant squashed the house with his foot.
The: definite article, qualifying 'giant'
incredibly: adverb of quantity, modifying 'enormous'
enormous: adjective, descriptive, qualifying 'giant'
giant: noun, common, singular, common gender, subjective case, subject of 'squashed'
squashed: verb, past simple tense, third person, singular, finite (subject = 'giant'), transitive (object = 'house'), regular conjugation, indicative mood, active voice
the: definite article, qualifying 'house'
house: noun, common, singular, neuter, objective case, object of 'squashed'
with: preposition, governing 'foot'
his: possessive adjective, qualifying 'foot'
foot: noun, common, singular, neuter, objective case, object of 'with'

24 The Goblin told the Hobbit that his feet were too hairy.
Principal clause: The Goblin told the Hobbit
Subordinate clause: that his feet were too hairy (noun clause, object of 'told')

Books for further reading and exercises

- Isobel Woodside, *Go for Grammar*, Rigby Education, 1979
- Excel Basic Skills series and Excel Essential Skills series (English grammar, punctuation, spelling, comprehension and creative writing workbooks by various authors, for primary and secondary school students). Published by Pascal Press
- Peter Howard, Basic Skills series (English grammar, vocabulary, creative writing, spelling, punctuation and comprehension workbooks for school-educated and home-educated children from preschool to late secondary). Published by Jim Coroneos
- Brian Bailey, Virginia Shaffer and Harry Shaw, *Handbook of English*, McGraw-Hill, Sydney, 1968

Notes